PRACTICAL GAS FLOW

PRACTICAL GAS FLOW

Techniques for low-budget performance tuning

JOHN DALTON

MRP

MOTOR RACING PUBLICATIONS LIMITED
Unit 6, The Pilton Estate, 46 Pitlake, Croydon, CR0 3RY,
England

ISBN 0 947981 33 0
First published 1989

Photoset by Tek-Art Ltd, West Wickham, Kent

Printed in Great Britain by
The Amadeus Press Limited, Huddersfield, West Yorkshire

Contents

Introduction

It seems, looking back, that I have always had a strange fascination with trying to make things go faster. One of my first memories is of an aeroplane trying to catch a 'doodlebug' (a V1 flying bomb). I wondered why it couldn't, so I asked, and I vowed that one day I would make one that could. I never did, of course, but for weeks I spent every spare moment drawing aeroplanes with bigger and bigger propellers, and with smaller and smaller wings; I even 'invented' contra-rotating props before abandoning the idea due to lack of funds. Then came pressed-tin clockwork cars and Meccano dragsters and model aeroplanes powered by penny rockets and all sorts of weird and wonderful creations.

I suppose my first real 'tuning' – I use the term very loosely – was on my father's Cyclemaster, a 25cc two-stroke engine in a special wheel that fitted in place of the normal rear wheel in a bicycle. I polished the ports, raised the compression ratio, fitted a trumpet on the carburettor and, the most magic part of all, fitted a megaphone exhaust made from part of an old boy scout's bugle, and I actually persuaded my father to try it. To me it sounded just like a Manx Norton, but I don't think the neighbours would have agreed: anyway, we compromised and I made a straight-through absorbtion type silencer that was quieter than the standard item. But the best thing was that it actually *was* faster than other Cyclemasters.

That must have been when the rot really set in, because

there have not been many vehicles that I have owned that haven't had their innards interfered with in some way or another. By this time I had, to my teachers' relief, left school and was an apprentice in a garage with day release to the local Technical College which gave me more people to plague with questions. I started to read all I could about the subject of power output, especially how to increase it, and found to my surprise that, although there were a lot of things everyone recommended, once you got past the basics there were an awful lot of contradictions in print. My early efforts, like a lot of other people's, were noisy and difficult to ride or drive, though I kidded myself that I had improved things.

Then I got involved with Air Force jet engines and really started to learn about air and gas flows and also how they work in the practical world outside the laboratory. Once you get inside, you can see from the various stains on blades, ducts and combustion systems how the air or gas actually flows when they are in use. It was obvious whoever designed them knew an awful lot more about gas flow than I did. So I set about finding out how jet engines really worked as opposed to how I thought they worked, with the idea of transferring my new found knowledge across to motorcycle and car engines. It soon became clear that, because the manufacturers were still learning (and still are), it was going to be an uphill struggle; the people who knew the answers wouldn't tell, but there were lots who told but didn't! So I started on a long, very long, period of experimenting which, after false starts and wrong directions, led me eventually to the system outlined in this book. In the meantime, of course, other people had also been experimenting, and on bigger budgets, and some of their ideas are actually in production so I have been able to adopt those too, once I have proved them.

During my research the theory sometimes only arrived after the practical proof, as is often the way in life – after all, the universe had been around a long time before people like Albert Einstein proved why it should be. I suppose, despite my previous comments, that being basically a nuts and bolts man has always tended to make me somewhat suspicious of pure theory. But also being (I hope) practical, I have realized that to gain the most benefit from something that works I should know why it works, if only so that I can refine it or use it in a completely different application. Having said that, I am not intending to try and baffle you with figures or weigh you down with lots of theory. In the early stages I nearly drove myself and a few other people mad with all the mathematics and formulæ involved. Eventually I realized that much of it was unnecessary, even in some cases misleading. Perhaps it's because what we are working on hasn't always read the text books. By all means get yourself a book on fluid mechanics, it will help your understanding. In *this* book, however, we will stick to the practice of being able to see and measure results. After a while you too will develop the knack of being able to see potential problems just by looking for them.

For quite a long while I intended to keep the whole system to myself, not even revealing all to close friends. However, when the after-market tuning business really started to boom, I realized that a lot of people wanted a bit more than standard performance. Likewise it dawned on me that there must be many others who, like myself, cannot afford the king's ransoms that are being asked for some of the goodies but who, with the right guidance, wouldn't mind doing a bit of work to finish up with something that really can be better, with the added satisfaction of having done it themselves.

Before the emphasis on low-budget, practical solutions leads anyone to think I am anti high-tech, I had better say that I am not, it's just that my view of it is not quite the same as the salesman's or the glossy brochure. I believe in sound basic design, not mediocre design sorted out by a microprocessor or other devious means, and certainly not poor design disguised for the market-place by unnecessary gadgetry. I do think computers have their place in cars, as the only sure way to control ignition, for instance, and probably fuel injection too.

As you will have deduced by now, it's the top end of the engine, the cylinder head, inlet tract and exhaust system, that I've mainly focussed my attention on here. My assumption is that you, like me most of the time, are stuck with an engine that wasn't made with high performance as the first consideration in its designer's mind. Consequently working on the cylinder head can be a bit like the old man, who, when asked the way, said, 'If I was going there I wouldn't start from here.' In other words a degree of practical compromise is called for. If you can afford four-valve heads and turbos you probably won't be reading this book anyway – if you can and you are then I'm flattered. Not that the system doesn't work on high performance engines, it does, though, as mentioned later, it is a matter of diminishing returns. So this is not a book on how to design cylinder heads, if it were I wouldn't start from here!

This book does not assume that you have large sums of money to spend on improving your car, though inevitably there does come a point when some expenditure is required to make progress. For example, I really can't recommend do-it-yourself camshaft reprofiling – though, like most things, it has been done! But it does assume that you are familiar with the workings of the petrol engine and possessed of a reasonable degree of mechanical aptitude and manual skill. The methods described will demand a considerable measure of care, patience, persistence and time, but they also offer a great deal of scope for learning as you go along.

What follows is certainly not a specific set of instructions for one engine or one predetermined end result. Rather, it provides a method which you can adapt to your own requirements, letting you proceed at your own pace, as boldly or as tentatively as your inclination and circumstances dictate. The important thing is that you are able to experiment systematically, checking and understanding the effect of each modification, so that you can chart your own course and decide your own priorities. Not everything suggested is applicable or desirable for every engine. But as you pick and choose it's important to remember that modifications to one part will probably highlight deficiencies elsewhere and maintaining the overall balance is essential. With that in mind, do please read the whole book before embarking on any work.

Good luck!

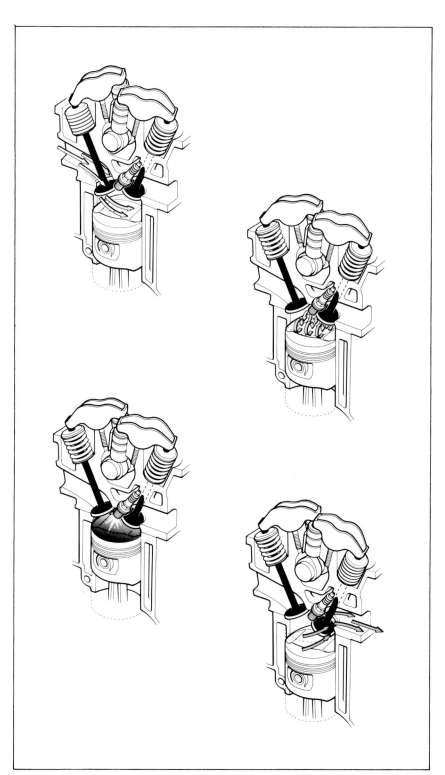

The four-stroke cycle. Improving gas flow into and out of the combustion chamber, so that the cylinder is filled and emptied more effectively, is the key to raising the volumetric efficiency of an engine and hence its power output.

Preliminaries

Because the designers of any mass-production car have to consider many factors other than maximum performance, not least the limits set by the cost accountant, it is almost always possible to increase the power output of a particular engine by giving it the attention the factory cannot afford. Improving its volumetric efficiency by optimizing the gas flow into and out of the combustion chambers is the principal means available to the tuner. A relatively cheap and simple test rig and some ingenuity will let you study that gas flow and find out how to modify it. But before you set about transforming your engine into a fire-breather, there are some basic points to think about.

Although this book is intended as a poor man's guide to engine performance it must be admitted that to improve performance you will have to spend some money. However, as the biggest part of the cost of any item these days is the labour charge and this you will be doing yourself, it will work out considerably cheaper than if it were possible to buy the equivalent modified parts. I also think that with my guidance and your hard work and persistence you will end up with an engine that is better than if you bought all the parts and just bolted them together.

There are a number of important points that you should bear in mind before you start. Firstly, PLEASE make sure that your car is capable of handling the extra power you intend to bestow upon it. Don't forget brakes, steering and roadholding. Your own safety as well as that of others could be at stake. It's no fun, either, to discover that you cannot use all that hard-won power because the suspension, tyres and so on are not up to it. So before you tune the engine sort the car out.

The second point, and this one I learnt the hard way, is don't attempt to tune a worn engine, it's a waste of time and effort and will only lead to disappointment. Reconditioning your engine if necessary is best done by a small local workshop; you can explain that you intend to tune the engine and would like everything to close tolerances. Many small workshops (but not all) tend to be run by enthusiasts who will go out of their way to help, even searching through catalogues for things like heavy duty bearings which will fit your engine. Don't forget, though, that they are in business to make money so it might cost a little more or at least deserve a tip.

The next point is being sure of what you want before you start. There is no point in producing a racing engine just to toddle around town. If you follow the words and music in this book you should end up with an engine that is still reasonably flexible but with lots of get up and go. But forget caravan or trailer towing, for example: for that you need a different power curve altogether. My assumption is that you are aiming for what is loosely termed a fast road engine which, if used normally, will equal standard mpg figures. Peak power is by no means the only consideration, as without a usable spread of torque a car can be misery to drive. If, on the other hand, it is a racing engine you are after, most of the techniques will still apply, with some changes in emphasis and some extra work discussed later in the book.

A lot depends on the design of the particular engine you are working with. The tuning system I have devised has worked for me on quite a wide selection of engine types from relatively 'cooking' pushrod units to more sophisticated twin-cam motors. But it cannot overcome basic design limitations like siamesed ports, though it does help. What I am trying to say is that you can't make a silk purse out of a sow's ear – improvements, yes; miracles, no.

Conversely, there is also a law of diminishing returns which is applicable here. It's often easier to extract a 50% power increase out of an ordinary engine than 25% out of an already well developed and highly tuned one.

Bearing this in mind, it's possible to modify the head of an originally low-stressed engine to produce so much power that you can wreck the bottom end. So unless you can afford a steel crank, special con rods and pistons, and so on, it's best to stick to the original red line on your rev counter. Highly stressed parts such as big-end nuts and bolts should be renewed as a matter of course anyway. When considering the suitability of a particular engine for improvement, the range of parts and modifications on offer from the tuning firms who advertise in the motoring press is often a good indication of where possible problems might lie.

Power and its production

At the risk of repeating what everyone else has said on the subject of power production, I still think it's worth going over the fundamentals briefly again. There are three main factors which determine the amount of power produced by an engine. They are the mechanical, thermal and volumetric efficiency.

Mechanical efficiency is fairly self-explanatory: basically it means how much of the push on the piston exerted by the expanding gas comes out at the flywheel. There is not much you can do about improving this apart from being as meticulous as possible when rebuilding the engine; however, a bit more later on this subject.

Thermal efficiency means roughly speaking how much of the fuel burnt in the cylinder actually pushes on the piston as opposed to heating the exhaust and radiator. Once again this is not very easy to improve on, due to the very nature of the petrol engine. Incidentally it's worth pointing out that when you hear thermal efficiencies of 20% or less being quoted it is probably absolute zero temperature that is being used as datum. Increasing the compression ratio is one way of improving things in this department but there are snags. Again more later.

So, of the three, this leaves us with volumetric efficiency – fortunately this is where we can go to town. If you regard an engine as a complicated air pump, then you will see what 'volumetric' means. An efficient engine will be capable of consuming (or pumping) more air and therefore more fuel than an inefficient one, thereby being able to exert more push on the piston. However, an engine is not in practice just an air pump, and if you start to think of all the variables, you can see how complicated things can get. Nevertheless, if you will bear with me and read through the book before starting anything, you will understand what to aim for.

It is possible to design a normally aspirated engine that has a volumetric efficiency of more than 100%, although to be fair this will usually only be achieved at relatively high crankshaft speeds over a very narrow rev band – at other speeds the efficiency would be very low. The old Manx Norton motorcyles were typical examples, with high-lift, wide-overlap valves, ram inlets and tuned reverse megaphone exhausts. They were somewhat unkindly known as constant speed variable noise engines, but in the 1950s they were producing around 110-120bhp per litre which isn't bad even by today's standards. For road use, though, as well as for many forms of competition, there are other things to be considered as well.

Before we get into improving the breathing of your engine in particular, a little talk on engines in general and what you need to start your modifying will be useful. From a performance viewpoint, modern production engines are quite well designed and getting better all the time. For any engine tuner, amateur or professional, this means more work: the old days of a quick clean out of the ports with a rotary file have long gone. Although to a certain extent it still works, you would probably find that a free flowing air filter and exhaust would do better to start with.

However, mass produced engines all suffer to some extent from a disease called 'productionizing'. This, put simply, is the difference between what the designer would like and what it's possible to produce economically. Very few manufacturers can afford to hand finish ports and so on. I am not including exotic marques in this, but even they are not immune – after all, they have to make a profit to survive. Once prestigious names that have disappeared or are now just badge engineering prove this.

What about blueprinting? Well, if you are restricted by the rules of a competition formula it can help, but it doesn't overcome basic production compromises and it can cost a small fortune to have done.

To recap, an engine produces power by burning a petrol-air mixture (approx 1/15 ratio by weight) in the combustion chamber and cylinder, producing heat and therefore rapid expansion. The piston and everything below it convert this expansion into rotary motion to be transmitted to the wheels. Assuming a reasonably constant thermal efficiency, the more mixture you can pack into the cylinder the more power you produce, it's as simple as that!

One way is to fit bigger carburettors, bigger valves and a camshaft with longer opening periods. But if you go too far the engine becomes very inflexible and difficult to live with, especially in traffic. The manufacturer might, before this point is reached, be inclined to fit a low-boost turbo as it can

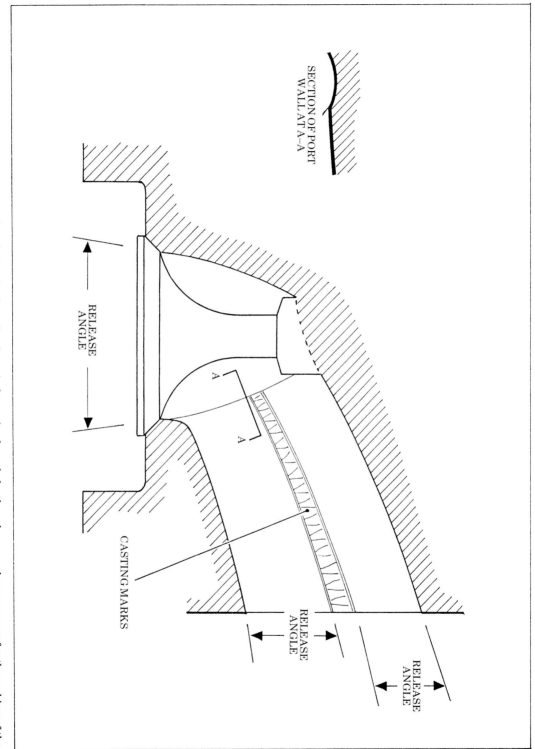

Fig 1. Section of a typical inlet port as produced, showing how the shape is determined partly by the release angles necessary for the making of the casting, not purely by considerations of gas flow. Casting marks and abrupt transitions from one section to another are other examples of the compromises resulting from rapid mass-production. To eliminate or rectify such 'productionizing' would be far too costly for the manufacturer on the vast majority of engines; the tuner, on the other hand, able to spend far more time on a single unit, can aim for much higher standards of finish.

15

overcome a lot of problems all at once and at the moment it's also good badge engineering for the market-place. Another way, of course, and one that you can do yourself, is to fit a bigger engine. More subtle than any of these additions or substitutions, however, is to improve the breathing of the engine internally and for that we need to cure it of 'productionizing' and other problems.

Cylinder heads, being castings, have to contain draft or release angles in the core pattern. With well thought-out designs the meeting points of these angles will mostly be in the least obtrusive places (although not always), but they are still there. Also, due to production tolerances, ports do differ in their internal finish: if any machining is done it's usually confined to the valve throat and manifold face end. With the majority of engines in everyday use this is quite adequate and any further work would be an unjustified expense.

As already mentioned, you can improve things slightly by removing the rough finish and the obvious bottle-necks. This is usually called stage 1 tuning. Or you can go further and fit bigger valves and really open up the ports, stages 2 and 3. But this is where things can and do start to go wrong: it's very easy to finish up with an engine that's inflexible, drinks petrol and isn't much quicker than normal.

What you have to do is match everything you fit or modify, from the air inlet to the exhaust outlet. Professional tuners use a flow bench which accurately measures flow rates through all the ports and passages – the only problem is that such equipment costs a small fortune. However, do not despair, because we can do almost as well – in fact, if we are really sneaky, even better.

Think of the humble vacuum cleaner, what does it do? It sucks air and so does an engine, so why not use one as the basis for a flow rig? I don't suggest you use the family one, though. I did once and was in trouble with my wife, she accused me of ruining it! Scan your local newspaper and corner shop window adverts and I am sure you will find a suitable bargain. The ideal is a cylinder type that you can still get spares for.

You will also need a vacuum gauge reading from zero to 10in water and a manometer which you can make yourself. If you can't locate a suitable vacuum gauge another manometer can be used but for safety reasons a gauge is preferable, the reason being that you will be measuring vacuum in the ports with the valves at different lifts and if you inadvertently shut one completely the fluid from the manometer will be sucked into the vacuum cleaner motor which is not a good idea.

Basic equipment

The basic things you will need to start with are shown in the accompanying illustration.

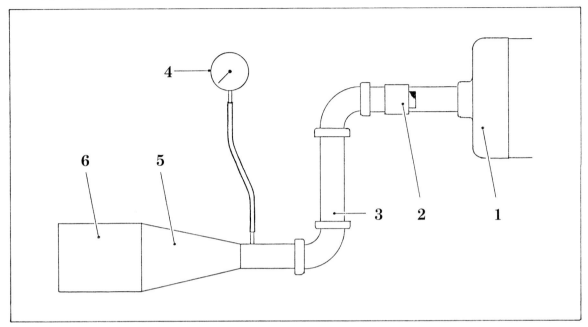

1: **Vacuum cleaner**. We have already discussed the best type: leave it as standard as possible just in case it needs replacing. All you need do is throw away the dust bag and filter and make an attachment for the next item.

2: **Variable bleed valve**. This is used to zero the system, using a datum-sized hole over item 6, and for varying the flow rate through the system. It's best made from a piece of sink waste pipe about 36mm internal diameter from your local DIY store. Cut a slot about 20mm square in this, then make a sleeve that fits over so you can vary the leakage rate (**Fig 3**). I used 0.5mm styrene sheet (available from model shops as Plasticard) warmed with boiling water, wrapped around and glued. It needs to be quite a snug fit. Make these parts as accurately as you can because you will be measuring the opening later to within a few thousandths of an inch for reference.

3: **Connecting pipe**. Ordinary cleaner hose will do but a better arrangement is the same pipe as the bleed valve using large radius bends (also from the DIY store), to get from the cleaner to the head.

Fig 2. Schematic layout of basic equipment for flow testing. 1: Vacuum cleaner. 2: Variable bleed valve. 3: Connecting pipe. 4: Master vacuum gauge. 5: Cone. 6: Dummy cylinder. The connecting pipe can of course be arranged to suit your particular working conditions, but try to avoid anything which will tend to restrict the air flow. The connection for the vacuum gauge tube should be flush inside the pipe to avoid a local disturbance which might give false readings.

IMPORTANT: it is essential that any engine parts connected to the test rig are completely free of petrol. A vacuum cleaner, like any other electric motor, may produce sparks at the brushes which could ignite petrol vapour with very dangerous results.

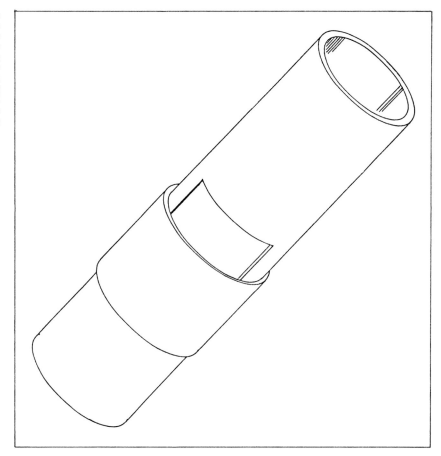

4: Master vacuum gauge. Connect this about 12mm inside
the parallel section behind the cone making sure that the joint
inside is flush. From here join up to the gauge using
windscreen washer tubing. The gauge should ideally be fixed
to something solid and somewhere easy to read.

5: Cone. This increases the diameter from the internal size of
the hose or pipe to that of the dummy cylinder. Again I use
0.5mm styrene sheet rolled and glued, but my very first one
was made from an old shirt box. The cone needs to be 2½ to 3
times longer than the bore diameter of your cylinders.

6: Dummy cylinder. Make this the same size as the bore and
stroke of your engine. Once more I used 0.5mm styrene heated
and rolled around a couple of old pistons. Make it several
layers thick as it needs to be as accurate as possible. Don't glue
it to the cone, hold it on with masking tape because you will be
needing this by itself later.

It goes without saying that everything should be as airtight as possible to avoid misleading air leaks.

Another very useful, I might say vital, piece of equipment is a vernier caliper for measuring bleed valve settings, valve lifts, port throats and a whole host of other things. Go for the best you can afford, with a depth measuring facility.

The next thing you need to make is a reference plate. From a piece of styrene sheet cut a hole as near to 25.4mm diameter as you can. Then with the equipment rigged up as close to the position it will be used in as possible, place the plate over the end of the dummy cylinder, switch on the cleaner and let the motor warm up. Take a note of the vacuum gauge reading and mark this on the plate. Now even if you have a disaster and have to change cleaners you have a basic reference point to come back to. For absolute accuracy you should also note ambient temperature and if possible barometric pressure.

That completes the basic equipment you will be using to test your engine's gas flow characteristics and experiment with improving them. You will be needing other bits and pieces but these are best described as we go along.

This differential pressure gauge, used as a vacuum gauge, is calibrated in inches of water and was bought very cheaply at a car boot sale.

2

First experiments

The vital functions of the equipment you have assembled are to let you compare results before and after alterations and to locate particular problem areas. Because it is an instrument of comparison, it does not need to be calibrated to measure flow rates in any specific units (though there is a way of doing that if required which is discussed later on). The first step is to test your engine and get a basic record of its gas flow in unmodified form. This will give you something to check the effect of future changes against. Then you can begin to explore the inlet tract to find out where the restrictions are. Better flow, remember, reduces vacuum.

If you can, before you strip the engine, measure the maximum lift on inlet and exhaust valves using your vernier caliper. It is possible to work these out if the engine is already a box of bits but it's not so accurate because pushrod engines very rarely have a 1:1 leverage ratio on the rockers and some OHC engines are very unhelpful in this respect especially those with hydraulic tappets.

When the cylinder head has been stripped and cleaned, refit all the valves minus springs, collars and collets. Lightly reassemble the inlet manifold, carburettor (**important**: make absolutely certain that there is no petrol in it) and air cleaner. Set the head up on your bench, valve heads uppermost, making sure you can reach underneath to move the valve stems up and down, and ensure that there is no obstruction of the air cleaner inlet. I now use a modified Workmate to hold heads but inverted T-shaped wooden stands do just as well. Whatever you use needs to be secure and firm – you won't get far if it keeps wobbling about!

Now open the carburettor butterfly fully and lock it there by any means that's convenient; compound venturi carbs need all butterflies open. SU and Stromberg constant vacuum carbs are a pest as the moving venturi portion needs to be held right up (without obstructing the throat) but I'm sure you can arrange something.

For the initial tests the exhaust valves need to remain closed. After fiddling around for ages, I eventually found that for all normal testing a smear of Vaseline (petroleum jelly) around the seat holds them in place.

Pop the inlet valves in, set them to maximum lift and hold them there with a blob of Plasticine wrapped around the stem and stuck to the guide and spring seat. Now position your dummy cylinder over the first combustion chamber as accurately as possible, there will be gasket witness marks on the head to help, then seal around the joint with Vaseline. Don't forget to put some spark plugs in, by the way.

Switch on, let the motor warm up and note the master gauge reading: depending on cleaner power, port size and valve lift this could be anywhere between 5 and 9in of water (incidentally inches of water give more sensitive readings than inches of mercury and so are better for our purpose). Now repeat this for all the remaining cylinders and note the figures down. It's a good idea to make another plate with a hole in which gives the same average reading for future reference, so you can see how things have improved.

Beginning flow checks
You are now ready to start your first flow checks, the object being to find out where and what the major flow restrictions are. It is a long winded job (no pun intended) but the more figures you collect the better, so keep at it.

Keep your set up as in the previous section, then, working on one cylinder at a time, slowly open each inlet valve (use your fingers) until you get the lowest gauge reading. Depending on your engine the first 1 to 1.5mm extra lift will give a drop but maybe after that, nothing. This means that your engine will benefit from a high-lift camshaft even if you do nothing else. So at this stage send off to all the reputable camshaft reprofilers for details of cams they sell for your engine; we will deal with camshafts in more detail later.

The second experiment repeats the first but without the air cleaner. Note down the figures of required lift for maximum flow. Thirdly repeat again with the carburettor/s removed, then finally with the manifold removed, noting the readings in each case. With the figures you have collected it's possible to start analysing the gas flow through the inlet system.

Removing the air cleaner will show you how efficient, or otherwise, it is. You can if you like divide this experiment in two, one with the air cleaner complete and the other with the element removed. If your filter system turns out to be a real flow stopper (and some are horrible) then a good aftermarket one is worth thinking about.

When you remove the carburettor it will show if that's a major restriction. If it is, then most cars either have or have had a sporty or GT version with improved carburation which you might be able to pick up second-hand. There are conversion kits available too but they tend to be expensive. However, in my experience it's not usually the carburettor that's the limiting factor unless your engine is very undercarbed to start with. If you have twin carbs or a compound carb already then certainly save your money until later.

In the third experiment, with the carb off, you will be able to establish the restriction and distribution qualities of your inlet manifold. Some are very good (Ford GT items for instance), others do tend to restrict a bit; once again, more later. Now, in the final experiment, if the improvement in flow rate continued up to the extent of a high lift cam then your ports are already quite reasonable, but we can do better!

By now you will have a fairly good idea of what limits the breathing and therefore the power output of your engine. It depends on your budget, but a better air cleaner and a high-lift cam are the main expenses you might have found necessary so far. It's obviously better to design your engine round the best you can afford.

3

Modelling

Particularly if you have never done it before, setting to work on your one and only cylinder head can be a daunting prospect. Supposing you discover too late that your modifications have been going in the wrong direction? Wouldn't it be nice if you could have a trial run first? How can you try out something that might be a good idea but might not? You could of course buy a spare head casting or two, perhaps from a scrap yard, to experiment with. But there is a cheaper and more versatile alternative, using a material much more easily worked than iron or alloy.

Having begun to establish which parts of the inlet tract, and in particular the cylinder head, are limiting the breathing of your engine, it's time to take a first look at the ways in which they can be improved. The basic technique is to modify the internal shape and finish of the port by grinding or filing metal away, and we shall be looking in more detail later at how to determine how much and where. It is possible to begin at once, working directly on the cylinder head. However, that is not to be recommended, mainly for the obvious reason that it's relatively easy to cut metal away but rather more difficult to put it back! Particularly in the early stages, while you are still learning, it would be all too easy to ruin the head and with it your budget.

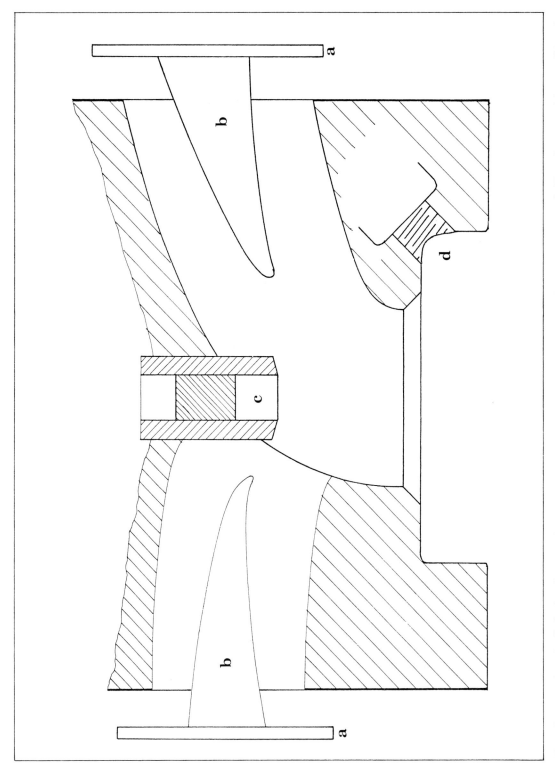

Fig 4. Cross section of cylinder head prepared for mould making. The manifold faces are closed by plates (a) extended into the ports with cones (b) made of wood, body filler or some other suitable material. The valve guide (c) and sparking plug opening (d) are sealed with Plasticine. Surfaces to which the silicone rubber might stick must be thinly coated with a suitable release agent.

Instead, I suggest that you make a plaster model of the head for one (or more) cylinder position, faithfully duplicating the original, and do all your flow testing and experimenting on that. If you do go wrong you can refill with plaster, or even make a new model, and start again. It also allows you to try out some pretty radical modifications with no risk of wrecking a head casting. Then, once you have achieved the desired result, you can copy the modified model exactly back onto the real cylinder head.

What you do is to take a moulding of the internal shape of the combustion chamber and ports and then use that to cast a plaster replica of the head – or the part of it we're concerned with, anyway. How easy or difficult it will be to do this depends partly on the shapes of the particular head you are working on, but a careful, methodical approach will usually get you there without undue heartache. For complete accuracy, the model needs to include both inlet and exhaust ports, so that you can examine every stage of the flow. In practical terms, though, the exhaust ports on many engines are already quite good and need little attention. If your early tests indicate that this is true of your engine, the modelling process can be simplified a good deal by omitting the exhaust port and moulding the chamber with the exhaust valve shut.

Should your first tests have shown up a big difference in flow between different cylinders, it would be a good idea to make models of the best and worst as a step towards the goal of equally good flow in all.

The first step in making a model requires a mould of the ports and combustion chamber. For this you will need some silicone rubber. There are a bewildering array on the market: the best I have found is Silcaset (the white variety) but any self-curing softish type will do. I suggest you look in the Yellow Pages for Strand Glass Ltd and make enquiries. It is possible to use bath sealer or a similar air-curing silicone by building it up in layers but it takes ages and some of them need a release agent.

Start by coating the surfaces of two flat plates with Vaseline and clamping them up to the manifold faces (**Fig 4a**). Non-crossflow designs need only a single plate, of course. Incidentally it saves on rubber and more importantly makes the mould easier to remove if you fit two cone shaped extensions, **b**, (not too deep, though, or they won't come out). Plug the end of the valve guide with a small lump of Plasticine (modelling clay) and push this up the guide (using a valve stem) until is about 6 or 7mm below the port end, **c**. Fill the spark plug hole with Plasticine until it's level with the inner face of the combustion chamber. **Fig 4** should make this all clear.

When making any kind of casting, as we saw when looking at cylinder head production, it's the release angles which determine what is possible and what isn't. Conical or bell shapes work all right if you can arrange to extract the cast towards the wider end – just like tipping the sandcastle out of an old-fashioned seaside bucket. Parallel-sided sections, if they are not too long, maybe just possible with silicone rubber because there is a little 'give' in it even when set, but it's safest not to rely on it. Anything with an enclosed shape or inverse curves is not on and will have to be cast in more than one piece, the pieces being subsequently put together to form a complete shape.

Before going any further you must decide if a one-piece mould will do or if you are going to need a two or three-piece one. The problem is that all the rubber in the ports has to come out past the valve guide and through the valve throat. The tapered plugs can help but silicone rubber can be quite brittle and stubborn. I must admit I've wrecked a few and had to start again. On non-crossflow heads (but not with siamesed ports)

In preparation for taking a silicone rubber mould from this Ford 2-litre OHC head, the sparking plug hole has been plugged with Plasticine, the exhaust valve sealed in place with Vaseline and the inlet port closed with a flat plate clamped in place.

and some hemispherical heads you can sometimes get away with one-piece moulds. On crossflow heads two or three-piece moulds are usually required, although they can sometimes be done with fewer. I will have to leave this decision up to you as it depends on the detail shapes of the head you are working on. Obviously single-piece moulds are better – but not much good if you can't get them out! If you have siamese ports there's no choice, that section will have to come out from the manifold side of the head. The more of the siamesing you model the more accurate will be your flow checking, by the way.

Fig 5. Making a two-piece mould. The cylinder head is supported at an angle so that the first pouring of silicone rubber reaches the level of the valve guide (a). When the rubber has set, some indentations are made in the surface (b) and a release agent painted on before the second layer is poured in, so that the two parts can be separated in order to remove them from the head and subsequently re-assembled accurately.

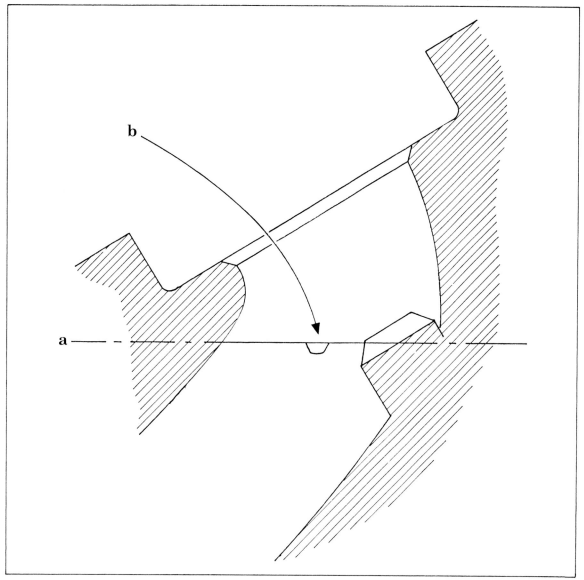

If you decide a two or more piece mould is required, proceed as follows. Prop the head at a 45-degree angle then, having mixed up enough silicone rubber, fill the port to the lower edge of the valve guide (**Fig 5a**). Incidentally when mixing and pouring silicone try not to aerate it, do everything slowly. Once you have poured it, tap the head repeatedly until all the bubbles are gone. When dry make some indentations in the rubber (**Fig 5b**); a 3mm drill used in your fingers will do, go in about 3mm. These will be registers enabling you to reassemble the parts accurately later. The next step is very important: with a modeller's paint brush, coat all of the exposed rubber with a suitable release agent, Vaseline thinned with white spirit or meths will do, so that the subsequent layer does not stick to the first.

Then repeat the whole operation on the other port. When they are both cured lay the head down horizontally, cylinder side up, and build a small dam of Plasticine, 6mm high is plenty, all round just outside where the cylinder registers are shown by gasket marks. Next mix enough rubber for the rest of the ports and combustion chamber and fill to just above the head face. It's worth mentioning in passing that silicone rubber can and indeed does disappear through the tiniest of holes, so make sure you haven't any leaks otherwise when you return to see if it's cured you could just find it all over the floor – again I speak with a certain amount of experience!

If yours is to be a one-piece mould it's still best to pour into

Pouring silicone rubber into the prepared combustion chamber and inlet port.

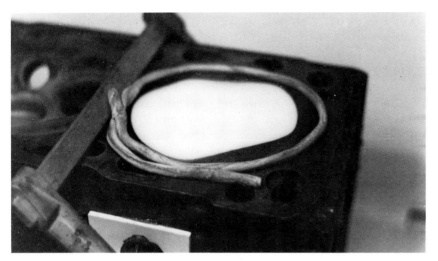

A dam formed with Plasticine serves to contain any silicone rubber which runs beyond the edges of the combustion chamber.

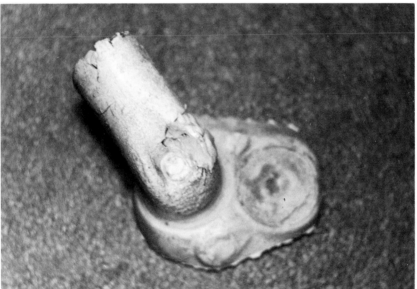

Top view of the rubber mould removed from the Ford 2-litre head. In this case only the inlet port has been moulded.

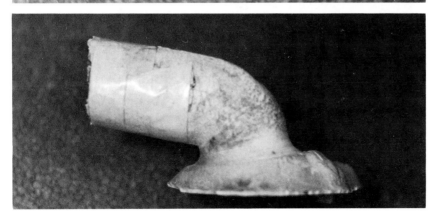

Side view of the Ford 2-litre combustion chamber mould. Note the sticky tape repair which is perfectly acceptable for this purpose, necessitating just a little extra work on the final plaster model – and that only if it is very rough.

the ports first with the head at a 45-degree angle, to avoid trapping pockets of air, before laying it down to complete the filling.

When all is cured the fun begins because removing the mould is a form of controlled vandalism. At first it will seem to have become an immovable part of the head but with firm and positive persuasion (and the right language according to your faith) it will usually come out with little or no damage. Minor damage can sometimes be repaired if it's nowhere vital.

If you have a more than one-piece mould now is the time to fix the pieces together. Some silicones will bond using a small amount of themselves as an adhesive; if not, bind them together using Sellotape. In either case it's important to degrease the parts completely before bonding them together to ensure a lasting join.

Making the model
Hopefully now you have a nice mould of the combustion chamber and ports to look at. However, there's not much you can do with it by itself although you might see some odd shapes that you didn't know were there. So on to the model, which we deliberately make in two or more parts. Firstly make a box out of anything suitable you have to hand, styrene sheet or compressed cardboard, with a suitable piece of chipboard for the base. Masking tape is ideal for holding it all together, it doesn't have to be pretty as it's going to be ripped apart shortly, see **Fig 6**. Attach the mould to the box using self-tapping screws at **a**; try to keep the ports level with the base. Next roll out two pieces of Plasticine, tapering them out from the valve stem diameter and fit them between the stub stems of the mould and the box edge. This side of the model doesn't need to be over thick, otherwise you will have problems moving the valves in and out.

On Plasticine, cardboard or wood you will need a release agent to stop the plaster used in the next stage from soaking in. Which conveniently brings us to plaster: you need a quick setting type which is runny when first mixed. I have tried all sorts from really thinned Polyfilla to dental plaster, but the best I have found is sold by model shops for the Linka Model house building system.

Having obtained your plaster, mix up enough to fill the box up to half the diameter of the first port (**Fig 6c**). Mix and pour slowly to avoid bubbles and air pockets. Before the plaster sets, tap the side of the box to help chase out any bubbles that might have formed. Don't worry too much about getting a smooth top

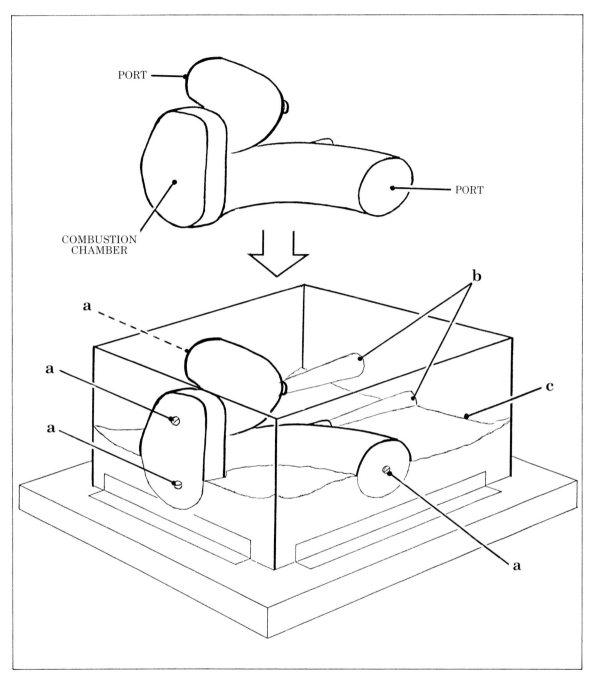

PORT

COMBUSTION
CHAMBER

PORT

b

a

a

a

c

a

Fig 6. Making the model. This example will be in three pieces; other shapes and valve configurations may be possible in two, some may even need more than three. The silicone rubber mould of the combustion chamber and ports is mounted in a box constructed of stiff card or other suitable material (shown ghosted here) and secured by self-tapping screws (a). Extensions (b) are added from the valve guide positions to the box wall. Plaster is first poured to the level of the centre of the lower port (c). Raised corners of the plaster form registers for subsequent re-assembly. When this layer has set and dried completely, it is coated with a release agent; the second layer is then poured to the centre of the higher port, and a third layer completes the model. Dismantling the box and separating the three sections, when set, allows the mould to be extracted, and the model can then be put together again.

The rubber mould attached
to two sides of what will be,
when completed, the stout
card mould box into which
plaster will be poured to
make the model.

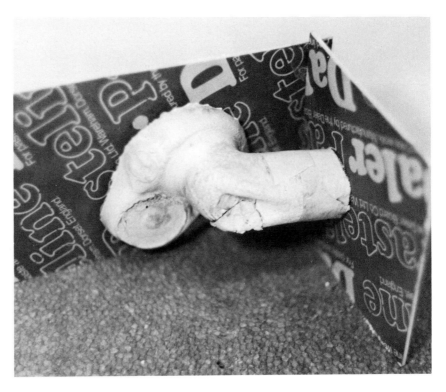

surface; in fact, just before the plaster hardens, you should lift
it in the corners to form a register for realignment.

Once the first pouring is dry, and this can take quite a while,
coat the plaster face with thinned Vaseline as a release agent.
Then pour in the second mix in the same way as the first, but
this time to half way up the second port. When dry pour
another mix, after applying the necessary release agent, up to
the desired height. Let the whole lot dry out completely
(preferably for 48 hours) then pull the box off. Gently prise the
casting apart and remove the mould. Now if you are lucky and
have been careful you should have an exact copy of your
combustion chamber and ports. After a few more small jobs you
will be able to really start work. Incidentally, hemispherical
heads and some others with valves in line across the head only
need a two-part casting, making life a little easier.

Now for the small jobs. First fill any air holes and repair any
damage to the castings (Plasticine can be used in air holes).
Then clamp the whole lot together and, using a flat surface,
sand the chamber side down to correspond with the level of the
cylinder head proper (production paper glued to a suitable
piece of chipboard works well). Insert the inlet valve, pushing
it right home, then pour a small amount of plaster to one side

of the stem thus giving it additional support (**Fig 7**). Now repeat this for the exhaust valve. If you have any problems getting the new plaster to stick, it could be that the original plaster is extracting moisture from the new so try prewetting the area. If that doesn't work Linka glue can be used to stick the new part in when set. That's the model complete and now the easy part's over, the real work is about to begin!

Fig 7. When fitting valves to the model head it will probably be necessary to add plaster to support the valve stem and keep it accurately positioned.

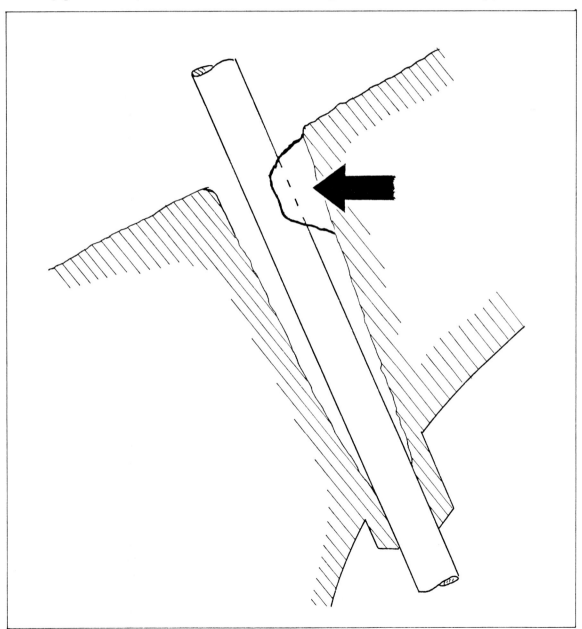

This is one half of a plaster model of the Ford 2-litre combustion chamber and inlet port, with the guide into which a real or dummy valve can be fitted. Note the four dimples made before casting the second half of the model to ensure that the two pieces can easily be aligned when assembled.

The rubber mould and one half of the plaster model of a twin-cam Alfa Romeo combustion chamber and inlet port. As with the previous Ford example, omitting the exhaust port simplifies the modelling process.

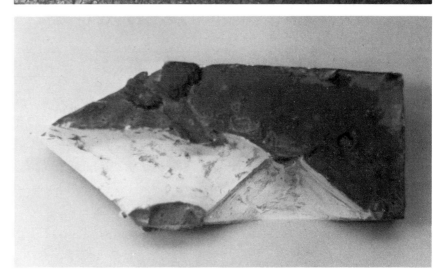

4

First modifications

Now that you have a replica of the cylinder head to work on, modifications can begin in earnest. The first and most obvious area to attend to is the inlet port, and the flow-checking technique will enable you to explore it section by section to locate restrictions. Achieving the best compromise in the area where the valve guide protrudes into the port is likely to be the trickiest bit. As the effects of improvements are cumulative and interdependent right through the system, you will probably come back to the inlet port again later, but the next in a series of possible things to look at is the inlet valve.

Before you start modifying, it's best to do a straight comparison check between the model and the real head. Set them up side by side and take readings from both inlet and exhaust valves on both the model and real cylinder head. Start with about 3mm valve lift and work up in 1mm stages until you reach the position of least resistance. You should find that they are identical; if not try to figure out why and rectify. Usually air leaks are to blame so try sealing the joints in the model with Vaseline. If it works all well and good but the trouble is it picks up dirt and dust and can be a real pain. At low valve lifts be careful not to shut the valve completely or you might wreck the vacuum gauge – it's much safer to set the bleed valve partly open to a known repeatable size.

Beginning with the inlet port

The first few modifications will be fairly standard ones. The most obvious one to try involves opening out the inlet port throat as shown in **Fig 8**. Cut back the plaster (file or sandpaper) until dimension **a** is about 1.5mm; you can go down to 0.75mm if you are after maximum performance but for a road car this could be too narrow, requiring constant valve grinding and adjustment. I have one engine that has done nearly 20,000 miles with 1.25mm valve seats without any problems, but some engines are notably prone to seat hammering and wouldn't do so well. When you have cut back the seat, for the moment just gently blend in at **b** and **c**. Do another flow check: you will probably find that the flow rate (decrease in vacuum) increases a little and continues right up to the lift for a high lift cam – that's good, and we haven't even really started yet.

Obtain a piece of thin wire (about 0.5mm) and curl one end into a loop of about 3mm diameter. Over this, roll a piece of Plasticine to make a 4.5mm ball. Now with the exhaust valve sealed shut and the inlet valve set at the proposed highest lift, attach the dummy cylinder and start to run the ball and wire up and down the port (with the cleaner warmed up and running of course). See **Fig 9**. Make sure your hand doesn't obstruct the airflow. You will probably have to make a bend in the wire to get all round the valve seat especially at **a** (a torch

Fig 8. First stages in inlet port modification. Narrowing the valve seat (a) allows the port opening to be enlarged slightly, (b) and (c).

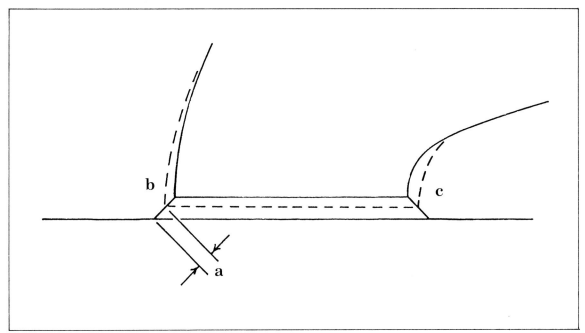

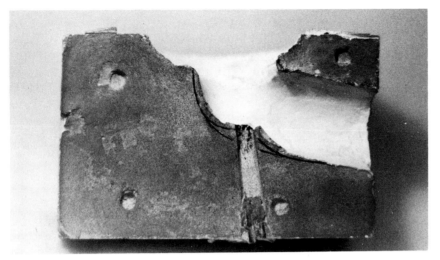

Half model of Ford 2-litre inlet port showing where plaster (and subsequently metal) is removed to improve flow by anything up to 15 or 20%.

Fig 9. Section of inlet port showing wire and Plasticine ball in use to check local variations in air flow. Marking a series of specific positions on the model, as shown here by numbered lines, enables you to make a coherent record of the readings taken.

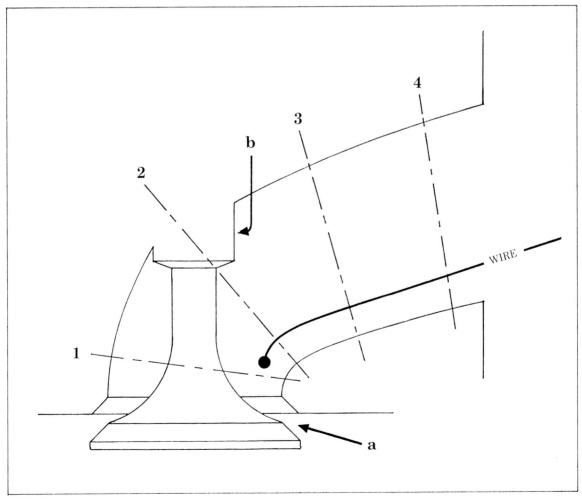

is helpful as it allows you to see exactly where the ball is). It's best to make some rough sketches of the port cross section, as in **Fig 9** and some circular sections at known distances from the manifold face, also marking them on the mould with a soft pencil. I would suggest four and one for the seat area should do.

Now take a series of readings with the ball at top, bottom and each side for each circular position. Then go on to the front, sides and rear of the valve guide, next do the same on the valve stem and all over the valve back, then finally all round the valve seat.

You should now have lots of figures. Anywhere (until you reach the valve opening area) where the ball increases the gauge reading (higher vacuum) represents in general terms a restriction. This can be slightly misleading, because the air is entering the port at the face and, as it doesn't want to go round the corner, it all heads for the far side of the port before going round the bend. So you have to bear in mind that you need to treat the top, sides and bottom as separate groups for the moment. The biggest restriction will be at the side of the valve guide whereas at **b** the ball will probably help spread the flow thus giving a lower reading (hint, hint).

This first experiment will show up major flow restrictions in the port itself, also it shows what a nuisance the valve guide is, and hopefully it will prove to you that most of the flow goes over the furthest side of the valve. If the readings are fairly stable try a slightly bigger ball of Plasticine until you are happy that you know where the problems are. Conversely if the readings are erratic and wildly different try a smaller ball.

Once you are happy that you know where the problems are, pull the model apart and, referring to your figures and sketches, start by removing any major port restrictions. Aim for smooth transitions and don't take off too much at once; retest and repeat as necessary.

Now for the protrusion of the valve guide into the port: you can if you like get rid of this completely which will improve the flow dramatically. However, it's not normally recommended for engines that have to do any great mileage as the remaining guide wears out very quickly, and because the valve seats have to be recut after guide replacement you will probably lose your thinner seats and finish up with pocketed valves which are bad news.

What is recommended is to streamline the existing guide in the direction of flow (**Fig 10**). Aim for the traditional tear-drop shape taking the sides down to about 1mm thickness. The trailing edge can be left blunt, **a**, as long as it's not too wide.

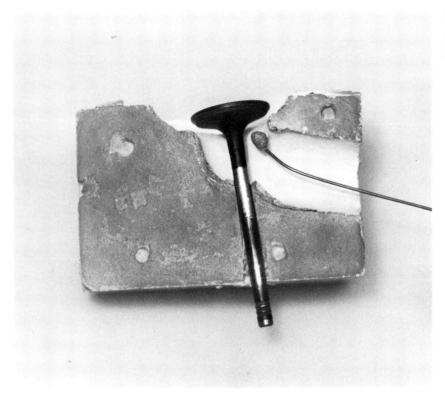

This is how the Plasticine ball is used to locate restrictions in the port when flow testing the complete model.

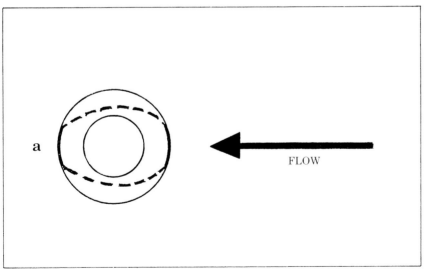

a

FLOW

Fig 10. The protrusion of the valve guide into the port can be streamlined along the direction of flow as shown by the dotted line.

Now reassemble and flow check again, noting any improvement. Also recheck the main port again; it's best to do this at each stage as you go along because as you improve things in one place you will find the restrictions tend to move about. Next, with a slightly smaller ball on a wire (about 2 to

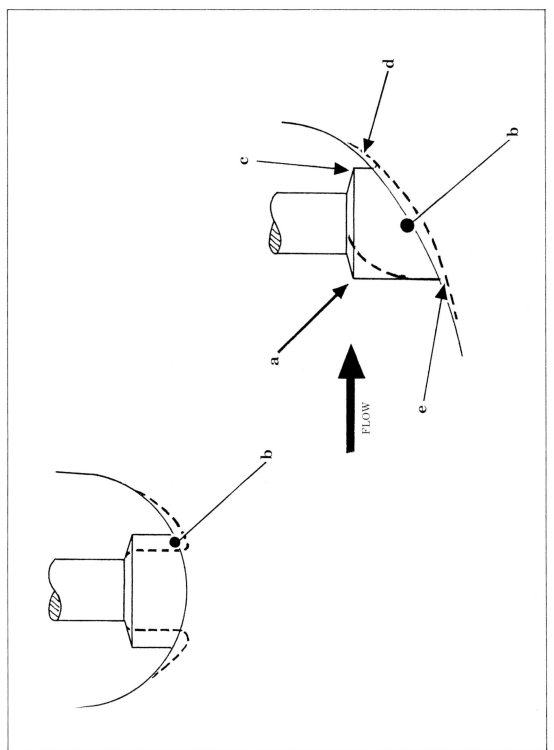

Fig 11. Side and end views of the valve guide in the inlet port. Flow past the guide can be improved by rounding off at (a) and blending the streamlining into the port wall, the hollows each side at (b) helping to compensate for the reduction caused by the guide in the cross-sectional area of the port.

2.5mm), check all round the new valve guide (**Fig 11**). You will find that **a** and **b** are the main problems. The first one can be improved by trimming down to the dotted line and then blending in to the tear-drop. If you don't go beyond the guide centre line it won't effect the wear qualities to any great extent. Don't worry about **c** too much, there's not a lot you can do and it's a relatively dead area: this you can prove yourself if you like by building it up with Plasticine. The flow at **b** can be improved vastly as in **Figs 11** and **12** by dropping the floor of the port as it passes the guide. It doesn't matter it you leave a tail as at **d**, **Fig 11** and **a**, **Fig 12** and a radius as at **e**, **Fig 11** and **b**, **Fig 12**. You can go down quite deeply here with safety (about 3mm). This is something that is reasonably easy to do on the model but is one of the worst jobs on the real cylinder head, a set of curved riffler files being the only real answer.

Do another flow test (you will begin to hate that expression soon – I never promised it would be easy!) By now you should have made a vast improvement, with a fairly steady reading on the gauge wherever you move the ball in the port (bearing in mind as always to treat top, sides and bottom as separate groups of the total).

I must admit that up until now we haven't done anything unusual that couldn't have been achieved by common sense and eye, it's just that we have been able to check flow rates and perhaps match things a little better. But from now on it's time

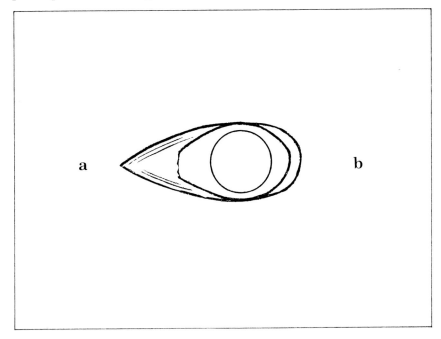

Fig 12. Where the valve guide merges into the port wall, the shape can be rounded at the front (b) and streamlined into a tail along the direction of flow behind the guide, (a).

Two views of an unmodified
Ford 2-litre OHC cylinder
head showing the protrusion
of the valve guide into the
inlet port as seen both from
the combustion chamber
and from the manifold side.

With Ford crossflow OHV
engines which have a flat-
faced cylinder head the
plaster model will replicate
the inlet port with no
combustion chamber. This is
a half model of a 1,600cc
version after modification.

Two rubber moulds show
the internal shape of a Ford
1600 crossflow inlet port
before (lower) and after
modification.

Cylinder head from a Ford
2-litre OHC engine after
modifications to the inlet
port, with the valve seat
narrowed and the valve
guide boss streamlined.

to get more technical and this is where the biggest improvements can be made.

Inlet valve

It is difficult to know in which order to start the next batch of modifications. It's very much a chicken and egg situation; if you improve the flow in one area the restriction moves somewhere else. You can chase up and down the port and valve modifying things only to find everything's moved elsewhere, so it's a real test of patience. However, if you follow the sequence as written I hope you will have less chasing as it gets the obvious out of the way first, but don't expect to get it right first time and don't neglect going back to basic flow checks occasionally.

Bearing these comments in mind we will firstly redesign the inlet valve. Once again it's a lot easier to work with a model. For this, use styrene sheet about 1.5mm thick filed or turned to correspond to the valve seat size. You can laminate sheet to gain thickness if needed. Glue on a dummy valve stem: you can obtain various sizes of styrene rod and tube but if you can't get any the required diameter, a piece of dowel sanded down or even a ball-point pen, in fact almost anything suitable, can be used. Use the real cylinder head as a jig to support the model while the glue sets and don't try to rush it, styrene solvent needs at least 24 hours to harden. When you are satisfied that it's solid, cut a hole in a piece of 1.5mm styrene sheet 3mm smaller in diameter than the valve head and attach this to the top face, when dry trim off down to the diameter of the valve head. Then cut out a disc about 7 or 8mm diameter and fit this in the centre. You have now made a 'penny on a stick' rimflow valve.

You can try it for flow if you like, it should be very good. But unfortunately it's not practical, because the real thing needs a radius behind the head to make it physically strong enough. This is where more experimenting is required. You will remember from your early flow checks that most of the air went over the far side of the valve: the idea is not to try and change that but to give a radius that hinders it as little as possible whilst giving enough strength to the valve. In the past, most valves were designed assuming that the gas flow had successfully turned the corner and was passing evenly over the whole diameter – unfortunately, as you have already proved, that isn't true.

For these experiments, build up the back of the valve with Plasticine. When you have finalized the shape you can copy it with car body filler. The shape to aim for is the best compromise giving the highest flow rate with the biggest radius; it will be a compromise, of course, just like everything else in a car. It will probably look something like **Fig 13** in cross section, the dotted line in this case representing the standard valve shape. Thinning down the valve stems, the part that's exposed in the port, might seem attractive but they really need to be made from better materials than a standard valve to retain enough strength, so I don't recommend modifying your own like that. Don't transfer the shape you have arrived at to the real valves yet as it might still need refining later.

The next point leaps ahead a bit but it's as good a place as

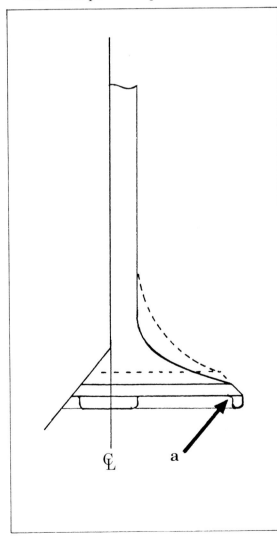

Fig 13. Half section of modified inlet valve, with the original shape shown dotted. The back of the valve is blended into the narrowed seating, and the cutout in the face at (a) aids flow past the rim.

45

any to mention it. It is difficult to make real rimflow valves without a lathe as the inner edge at **a** (**Fig 13**) needs to be quite sharp, but it can be done. Most of my valve shaping (if I couldn't use a lathe) has been done with the valve in an electric drill clamped to a bench (or the kitchen table if you are brave) using production paper wrapped round a piece of dowel to shape the back of the head. The rimflow portion can be done the same way once the initial groove has been cut. This is done with the drill on slow speed using the corner of a file very cautiously to start the cut, but please be careful. Some form of eye protection such as safety goggles is a sound precaution when embarking on such jobs.

The next step should really be the inner radius of the port but for the moment we will ignore it, coming back later when we have a better way of testing it.

Three views comparing standard and modified inlet valves (Ford 1600 crossflow) showing how the seat is narrowed, the curve behind the head reduced and the face inset.

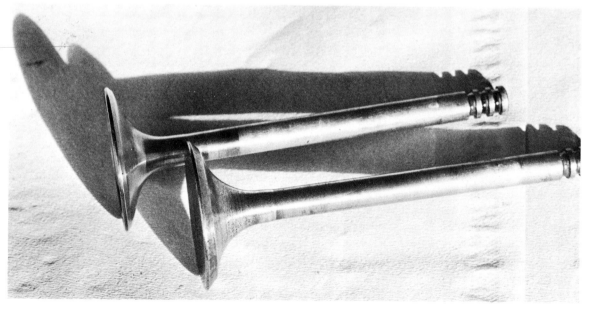

5

Further modifications

Improving the gas flow in the inlet tract in the ways described already is a sure way to increase the maximum power output of most engines. But there is a danger that the end result will be an engine with all its performance at the top end of the rev range and nothing lower down, which will make the car difficult and unpleasant to drive. A refinement to the flow-checking equipment allows you to probe local pressure variations more accurately and examine conditions at low and medium speeds. A more detailed picture of what is going on in the inlet port emerges, making it possible to tackle problems like flow separation in tightly curved sections. The exhaust port can be checked too.

The first engine I built using the methods so far described produced a lot of power but only at the top end. It wouldn't idle properly, was intractable and was generally a pain until it came on song on the high lift rally cam at about 3,500rpm. So I pulled it all to bits (well, the head anyway) and tried to improve things. To say that it took a lot of experimenting and analysing is an understatement. Some of the ideas I arrived at are now accepted practices but when I was developing the system I had never heard of them. And some of the ideas might seem strange but try them, I know they work. Eventually I got what I wanted. I still had a slightly lumpy tickover, but I could floor the accelerator at 1,000rpm in top gear and pull away smoothly until it reached 3,000rpm when it really began to fly. As a plus, it now produced even more power, bhp 30% and torque 20% up on the GT version of the engine using the same carburation.

To prove it wasn't a fluke the same system has since been used on a variety of engines and in every case it works, though admittedly for the diminishing returns reason mentioned earlier some engines will respond better than others.

When I first started to really analyse the flows through an engine I used some complicated mathematics, working out gas speeds in different parts of the ports and cross referring this to the vacuum cleaner flow rates and air speeds. You can do this if you wish (I will explain later a device for approximating the air speed in the port) but I don't normally bother any more as, by regulating the flow rate in the system with the variable bleed valve and using a probe, you can iron out most problems without having to resort to any maths. The only thing you really need to know is how the maximum gas speed in the port compares with the air flow speed generated by the cleaner.

Probing

I mentioned probing in the last paragraph and this is the secret, if any, for further development. The probe is simply a small-bore metal tube connected to a U-tube manometer. It can be used in much the same way as the ball of Plasticine was earlier but it's with other testing that it really comes into it's own. For the preliminary work the ball is better because it gives you the right information in the early stages.

Making the probe is very simple: it's just a length (about 250mm) of small-bore thin-walled metal tubing, a 2mm bore being about right. I used a piece of car radio aerial, bent round at the end to allow complete access. Model shops sell various sizes of tube which might also be suitable. Connect this to the manometer using windscreen washer tubing. The manometer is just a piece of 6.5mm bore clear polythene tubing bent into a U and held onto a piece of plywood by trapping between nails; a short piece of sink drain pipe at the bottom helps to make it neater. Fill it about halfway up with water coloured with cooking dye. You will also need a scale: mark this off in inches or centimetres according to taste (about 2in plus and minus). It should also be capable of being moved up and down so you can zero it. That's the manometer, see **Fig 14**.

Up until now you have been testing conditions at maximum flow rates but now you can test at lower air speeds. This

Fig 14. A manometer, simple to make from a piece of clear plastic tubing, is used to measure vacuum in the probe. The tube is formed into a U-shape round a piece of plastic drain pipe, can be fastened to a board with nails or staples and then is half filled with coloured water. One end of the U-tube is left open, the other connected to the probe. A scale is added against which the water level can be checked.

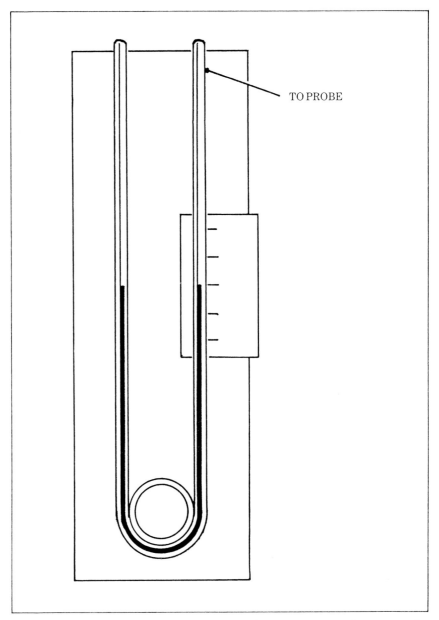

TO PROBE

equates more with conditions in the engine at low speeds, under partial load and also during acceleration. For this testing the procedure is slightly different. To start with, it's best to have the model and real head side by side for easy comparison. Arrange the real head with 2mm lift on the inlet valve, then by altering the bleed valve (obviously with the cleaner running) adjust until you have a reading of 1 to 1.5in showing on the main gauge. Now without altering anything (don't even switch off) transfer over to the model, also with a 2mm valve lift, where hopefully the reading should be lower, therefore proving that you have already improved things. Don't forget to make a note of the bleed valve opening.

Still working on the model, start probing down the port with your tube in much the same way as you did with the Plasticine ball. Now you can study the flow and speed more thoroughly, and begin to work out where problems might be occurring, by seeing what happens to the manometer reading. Continue to do this, increasing the valve lift by 1mm at a time, until you have reached full valve lift, resetting the main gauge to the first reference setting each time on the real head by altering the bleed valve.

Having made a little sketch of this lot, do it all over again using higher and lower readings on the master gauge thereby giving you higher and lower air speeds. A point worth mentioning is that although most professional flow checking is done at full valve lift, the valve is only in that position once during the inlet period; all other points the valve goes through twice, so any gains at partial openings will be doubly useful. Anyway, keep all the figures you have obtained safe for future reference. Some problems might show up at this stage so don't hesitate to try and cure them before going any further.

I think that now it's time to start on the inner radius of the port, I've been avoiding it long enough. First set the valve at full lift and, with the bleed valve fully open, start with the

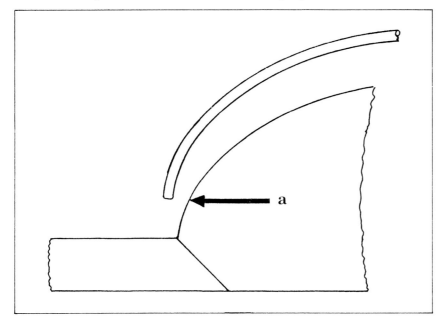

Fig 15. Using the probe to investigate air flow round the inner radius of the inlet port. At a critical point (a) where the curve sharpens the flow tends to break up into turbulence.

probe at the inner edge of the valve seat and slowly pull it back out of the port whilst watching the manometer for movement. Now slowly, in stages, increase the flow rate whilst repeating the probing. You will reach a point, **a** (**Fig 15**), when the manometer will start to fluctuate or do some very strange things. This means that the flow is breaking up or burbling: mark this point on the port with a pencil. Now make a little drawing of the curve, mark the point where the flow breaks up and record the vacuum gauge reading. Slowly increase the flow, noting the separation point and reading at each stage. Your drawing should now look like **Fig 16**. From this, you should be able to work out where to start your blending of the radius, the important thing being not to go back beyond **b** any more than you have to, this being the maximum flow separation point. As this is one of the most crucial places for gaining flow in the port it's worth spending as much time as you can here.

As you will get very small readings during this test (and also whilst the inlet valve is wide open) it can help to make another manometer and connect it into the main vacuum gauge line with a T-piece. By laying both the manometers back at an angle their sensitivity will be increased; a 45-degree angle will give you about a 50% increase. The further you lay them back obviously the more sensitive they become, but beware of water in your vacuum cleaner motor!

It will also pay you to repeat this test at different valve lifts. Some engines don't seem to be affected in this respect by

Fig 16. Use a diagram like this to record the flow separation points as the vacuum gauge reading, and hence the flow, is progressively increased. The maximum flow separation point (b) occurs furthest from the valve seat.

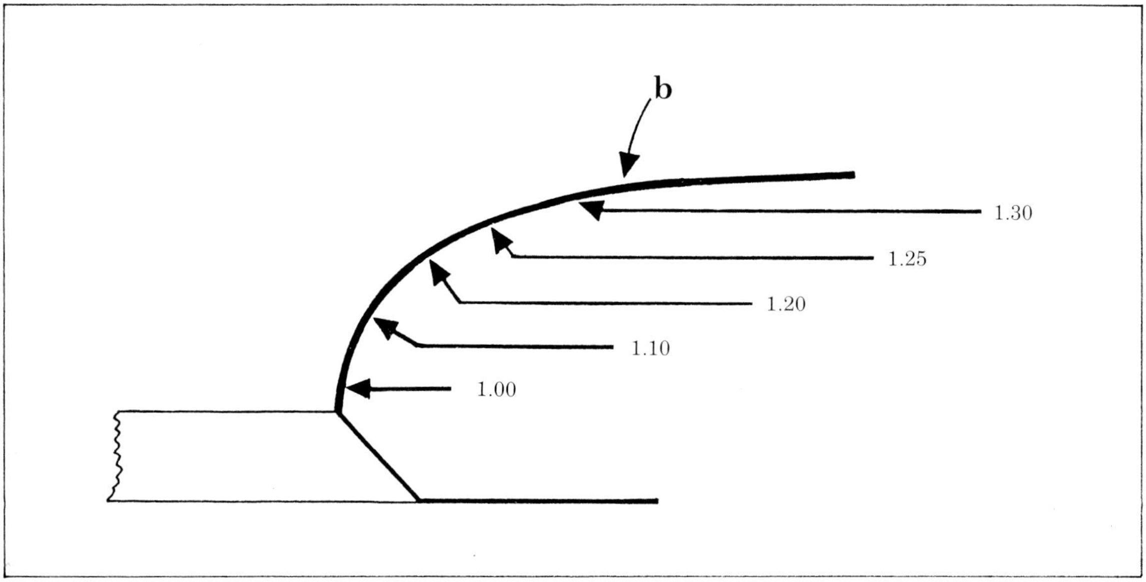

different lifts but others do.

At first sight it might seem that the shape shown in **Fig 17** would obviate the need to do all the previous work but unfortunately for a number of reasons it's not quite that easy. The first reason really has nothing to do with flow: the sudden increase in cross-sectional area could, at low flow speeds, cause the fuel to separate out of the mixture with all the problems that can create. If shortly I seem to contradict this statement forgive me – I will try and explain why the conditions are slightly different when we get there.

The second reason you will probably have guessed anyway. In your early tests you established that the majority of the gas mixture flowed over the far side of the valve. You can see by the arrow that cutting away the bottom would tend to send even more over the far side and even less round the inner radius. What we are trying to achieve is the utmost use of all the available valve area thereby increasing the total flow, not just improving it in one place.

Thirdly, especially on a head with valves in line, the extra flow going over the top of the valve would impinge either on the

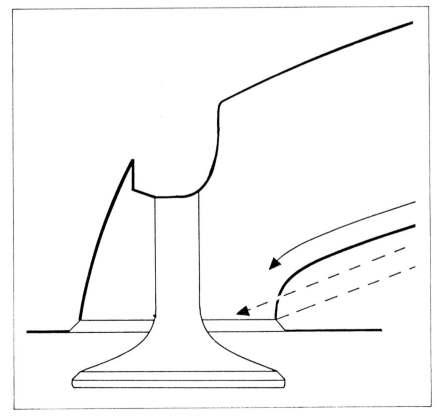

Fig 17. Straightening out the inner side of the inlet port, as shown here by the dotted lines, is not the answer to the problem of flow separation on the curve for several important reasons.

53

Fig 18. With some port shapes it is possible to exploit the venturi effect by opening up the outside of the curve (b) to discourage flow separation on the inside at (c).

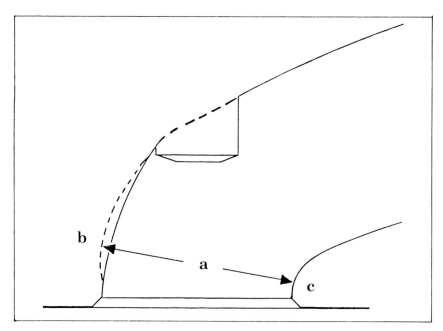

side of the combustion chamber (which would hinder flow) or straight onto the cylinder wall which is not only bad for volumetric but also thermal and mechanical efficiency (the latter because it would tend to distort the bore due to it's cooling effect).

But getting back to the radius, I know a compromise will have to be made because above a certain flow rate on some engines it doesn't seem possible to keep the flow attached as the radius is just too tight. However, there are a couple of little tricks that can help, assuming of course that you have already done your best with it before you go any further.

For the first, go over to the other side of the port and remove plaster as shown by the dotted line in **Fig 18** to a height of about 15mm. Go in to a depth of about 1.5 to 2mm and blend sideways into the main port shape after an initial central width of about 8 to 12mm (I'm sorry to be vague about dimensions but it varies with the port size). Now test this for separation round the inner radius, if necessary removing a bit more and so on until nothing more happens. If you do go too far then you will have to recoat with plaster and go back to the optimum. This modification will not make any real improvement at very low rates, and at maximum lift and high flow rate it might even cut the flow very slightly. However under all other conditions it should improve things dramatically. It does this by using the venturi effect at **a** to increase the local pressure across the port, thus tending to hold the flow closer into the corner at **c** because the pressure reads all the way over the width. Just before the valve seat the reverse happens, tending to eject the flow into the cylinder through the valve opening. This is the apparent contradiction about area changes I wrote about earlier. Try it for yourself and you will see that it works and, if you probe, why. Incidentally it helps specifically on Pinto inlet ports which are noted for their strange shape.

The second trick I have only needed to use occasionally and admit to doing straight on the head, usually in desperation. However, I will explain it and the reasoning behind it and leave it up to you to experiment. If you study a river and throw twigs in you will be able to see that the centre flows a lot faster than the edges. Air or gas flowing in a pipe behaves in a very similar way. This is known as 'Poiseville flow', the speed varying from maximum at the centre to zero at the walls. It is the virtually stationary gas breaking away from the completely stationary surface layer that initiates turbulence or burbling. Boundary layer turbulence can give a whole range of problems for people from designers of Concordes and Tornados to domestic plumbers. There are in the aerospace industry a number of ways to control and use it; most are

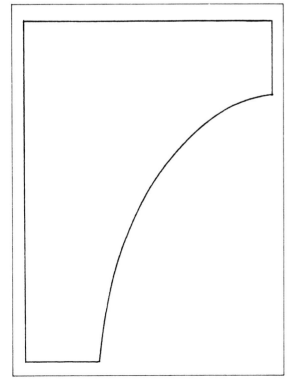

Fig 19. Example of template used when cutting curved grooves in the port wall to encourage tangential flow and discourage boundary layer turbulence.

initial design features but there are add-on types too. One thing they nearly all have in common is that they change the direction of flow in the critical regions just above the surface either by deflection or by creating vortices. Now by applying this idea to the inlet port perhaps you can see that what we need is either a lot of small vortices starting just upstream of the critical radius or to get the gas flowing tangentially round the radius. I have tried both but the second and simplest seems to work better. For this I used a series of spiral cuts starting about 12mm back from the radius at about a 40-degree mean angle, cut with the angled end of a scriber against a curved template, making the cuts about 1mm apart (**Fig 19**). As it worked in the situations tried I haven't really pursued the idea any further yet but I intend to when time permits. One point to remember is that some ports are offset to create swirl in the combustion chamber and your cuts should complement not oppose this, otherwise you might cure one problem only to create another.

By now you should have a very efficient inlet valve and port but at this stage I think it's worth going through the whole range of basic tests again at all flow rates and valve lifts. Note all improvements and check that it is not the main port that is now the major restriction: if it is, then remove as little as possible to balance things up.

Exhaust port
All the preceding work has dealt with getting as much mixture into the cylinder as possible and, although we haven't finished yet, perhaps before going on to make sure it stays there we ought to devote a little time to getting it out after it has done its work.

I think it's generally accepted that on a normally aspirated engine the exhaust valve should flow about 70 to 75% of the inlet flow and my experiments tend to agree. So if you now set up your equipment to check the flow by sucking OUT through the exhaust port some simple maths (and maybe an adjustable reference plate) will soon tell you what proportion you have. For this you will obviously need to make an adaptor allowing you to connect up to the exhaust manifold face of the head.

On most engines I have found the exhaust port to be reasonably efficient so that cleaning up casting marks, removing any obvious traps and pockets and maybe just slight streamlining of the valve guide gives the required flow. If yours doesn't come up to scratch then probe like the inlet port but remember the flow is out and under pressure. I don't recommend narrowing exhaust valve seats unless they are very wide because the seats help to dissipate heat to the cylinder head from the valve (they get *very* hot). One old dodge is to radius the valve edge and to make the face slightly convex, which will help flow slightly (**Fig 20**).

Incidentally you will have noticed that all the inlet testing took place on a fairly rough plaster casting, and from this you will deduce that I don't approve of highly polished inlet ports. In fact if you think of the boundary layer effect it's easy to see why. Tests do prove that a highly polished port flows less than a slightly rough one of identical shape – if you don't believe me try it yourself but do make sure that they are the same shape and size. The only thing polished ports do seem to do well is de-atomize the mixture at small throttle openings which is no help at all. The finish to aim for is a matt grey; if you cross hatch with 600 grade wet and dry you won't be far wrong. Believe it or not I have read only recently of one firm well known for cylinder head modifying who have just discovered this and are worried about how they are going to market non-shiny heads!

The exhaust ports, on the other hand, are a slightly different proposition. Flow is reasonably easy to bring up to scratch, so

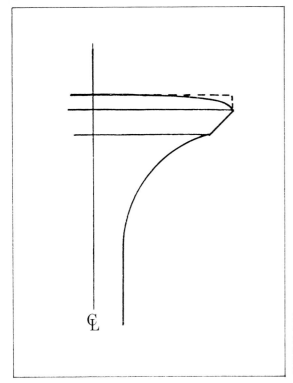

Fig 20. The seating of the exhaust valve should be narrowed only slightly if at all, but radiusing the edge to make the face convex will help to improve flow.

Modified Ford 1600 cross-flow cylinder head fitted with rimflow inlet valves and radiused exhaust valves.

no real problem, but you have a lot of very hot gas rushing through and the cylinder head is picking up heat all the time especially during acceleration. So working on the mirror principle of heat reflection, it's worth getting as high a polish on port and valve as possible in an attempt to keep heat soak to a minimum, thus keeping most of it, for the moment, in the exhaust gas.

6

Anti-reversal

Getting the mixture into the cylinder – and out again via the exhaust – has been the major concern so far: making sure that too much of it does not bounce back the way it came is important too! The behaviour of the charge travelling down the inlet tract towards the cylinder in the very rapidly changing conditions which prevail when the engine is running is sometimes less predictable than flow testing with a fixed valve opening might suggest. Work out how many times each cylinder is filled and emptied per minute at even quite modest revs to remind yourself that this is a dynamic system, not a static one. Valve timing is of crucial importance here. There are a number of possible modifications to help encourage flow in the right direction and inhibit its reversal.

Having done such a lot of hard work trying to get as much mixture into the cylinder as we can it's about time we put some effort into making sure it stays there. However, before we start anything a short and simplified discourse on valve timing might be a good idea to make it clear what you are aiming for and why.

As you probably already know, in the four-stroke cycle the exhaust valve opens before bottom dead centre (BDC) on the power stroke and closes after top dead centre (TDC) on the inlet stroke whilst staying open for all of the exhaust stroke.

Likewise the inlet valve opens before TDC on the exhaust stroke, stays open for all of the inlet stroke and closes after BDC on the compression stroke. **Fig 21** shows a typical valve timing diagram for a sports engine.

The main reason for all this (with the exception of early exhaust valve opening) is that gas when flowing possesses inertia, just as a pebble that is thrown has, or a rolling football or a car with no brakes. When not moving however, even with a push from behind it takes time to get going (just like me, especially on a cold winter's morning). If the valves opened and closed at top and bottom dead centre the engine would run, just, but very slowly and wouldn't be able to go much faster than a tickover. It's interesting to read very old books on motor

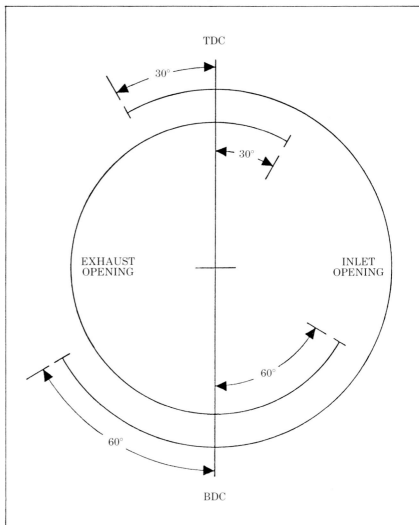

Fig 21. Typical valve timing diagram for a sports engine. Inlet and exhaust valve opening periods overlap symmetrically before and after top and bottom dead centre.

60

vehicle engineering and see the valve timings quoted and their operating revs.

If you imagine each cylinderful of mixture as a plug of gas travelling down the inlet system towards the valve then it's easy to see that it has inertia and that after BDC on the inlet stroke it will continue to try and get into the cylinder, even with the piston going up. The ideal is to shut the valve just before the piston starts to push it out again. Unfortunately this point varies with engine speed, at low speeds it's just after BDC whereas at high speeds due to the greater inertia of the gas it's obviously much later.

Going back to the opening of the valve, while the valve is shut the gas that was rushing in has been stopped and has built up presure behind it but has lost all of its speed and therefore will take time to start moving again once the valve begins to open. Once more it would be ideal to start opening the valve early, thus letting the pressure start to work, so that when the piston began to descend the gas was at full speed. Again, by opening the valve early enough that would theoretically be possible – as long as you only want to run the engine at very high and constant revs, that's if you could start it running in the first place! So the valve opening is a compromise just like the closing, and if you open it too early you will have exhaust flowing out of the inlet valve at low speeds.

A different but somewhat similar set of circumstances governs the exhaust valve timing, which I am sure you will understand if you study the four-stroke cycle and timing events. You will also understand what a difficult job the camshaft designer has, having to match not only the opening and closing to ensure they work at the same revs but also the inlet and exhaust to each other.

As you can see, the outcome of this is inevitably that valve timing is a compromise. If you have a lot of overlap at TDC and long opening periods your engine will develop power at high revs but not much at lower speeds. Pure racing engines take this to the ultimate so that some will not even idle and have to have their throttles 'blipped' to keep them running. Ordinary family saloons sometimes go to the other extreme, with small overlaps and short opening periods. This is very useful where the driver is reluctant to change down and will happily creep along at 25mph in top gear (usually in the middle of the road, but that's not really anything to do with the valve timing – at least I don't think it is).

Up until now you have been developing the head to flow as well as possible and if you just do this and nothing else your engine will be quicker. But, unless it's a high-performance engine you are working on, to gain the most you need a better camshaft and this is the next choice to make before you proceed any further.

If you haven't done so already I suggest you write to all the major camshaft regrinders and ask for full specifications of the ones they do for your engine. Most firms are only too willing to oblige, supplying all the details you require. What you need to know is:

1: How far open both the valves are at TDC on the inlet and exhaust strokes.

2: The overlap period in crankshaft degrees either side of TDC for each valve.

3: How far open the exhaust valve is when the inlet valve starts to open.

4: How far open the inlet valve is when the exhaust valve shuts.

5: The number of crankshaft degrees past BDC when the exhaust valve closes.

6: maximum lift of valve (or valves if they are different).

The rest of the cam design is obviously very important but here we have to rely on the cam designer's expertise. I recommend you go to one of the well known names. I have had excellent results from most of them.

As to which type of cam to choose, this is where you have to weigh up exactly what your car is going to be used for. Bear in mind that your modified engine will be more flexible than if you just fit the cam by itself, but the power and torque curves will be much the same shape though the outputs will be higher. For a road car I always go for the top of the range road cam which with my other mods means that I can toddle around if I feel like it but when I'm in a hurry I have to use the gears as they should be used.

Incidentally, do fit the camshaft exactly as recommended; check and double check that the timing is right, it's vital for success, especially as you will be arranging your ports to complement your cam. If you already have your camshaft make sure you know the figures you need before pulling the engine apart.

Going back to the business of valve timing, one result of the overlap we have already discussed is that before the engine has reached high enough revs for gas to flow in a sensible manner you will have a situation where the gasses can actually flow in the wrong direction, especially if it's a high performance engine with a radical cam. So now we will go on to devise and test every means we can think of (using a few that are now well established) to stop this reverse flow happening. You have already made a start with the rimflow inlet valve and the radius on the exhaust valve face. To be really effective the whole system should eventually be tested from air inlet to exhaust outlet, but for the moment we will concentrate on the cylinder head and its closest points.

The first thing you need to do is make an adaptor which will enable you to suck air through the inlet port (you should already have one for the exhaust port). Then you will need your dummy cylinder with a piston that you can set at TDC or further down as required.

Firstly, on the real head, set the standard valves at the opening which corresponds to TDC with your selected cam, and fit and seal the dummy cylinder and piston also at TDC. Take a set of readings with the flow in the normal direction (inlet to exhaust) by sucking through the exhaust port. Then swap the flow round, suck from the inlet port, and note the difference; do this first with the bleed valve wide open. Repeat for a variety of flow rates, increasing a small amount at a time from virtually nothing. The angled-back manometer is best for detecting and reading differences, as they may be small.

You will probably find there is hardly any difference in resistance for either direction on the standard head. Now remove the real valves and pop in your model rimflow valve and a modified exhaust valve and test again. There should now be a measurable difference, proving that the valve modifications work. Now try the same tests but with the valves at various lifts simulating the overlap period, not forgetting to move the piston of course! Do this with the modified valves, to gather data.

The next step is to repeat this all over again using the model, firstly with the standard valves then the modified ones. If you are lucky, because of the more efficient porting already gas flowed in the right direction the results will be better, if not don't worry, you have lots to do yet.

The mods I am going to suggest next could make me unpopular because they virtually ruin any chances of achieving ram inlet tuning by utilizing reverse pressure waves. I think, because anti-reversal allows longer valve opening periods with flexibility, it is ultimately capable of producing more *usable* power. Back to back tests tend to prove this, the tuned inlet only working at high revs over a very small band. We will discuss this again later. However, exhaust pressure wave tuning does still work, once again more later.

The first mod can be rather difficult to do on the model as it also involves the inlet manifold face. If you can, though, it's best done on the model first, if only so that you can measure what is happening before cutting the metal. **Fig 22** represents a cross section of the inlet system at the manifold face: rather than trying to match the openings as at **a** (dotted line), cut a taper as at **b** in the port opening all the way round. The dimension **c** should be about 4mm and the angle **d** should ideally be around 6 degrees. This works rather like a ratchet, allowing air to flow in one direction but forming a trap in the other; we will discuss the simplified theory behind it later. You can set up a double-direction flow test to optimize the size, probing so you can see what is happening.

Now turn your attention to the exhaust port. If you study **Fig 23** you will see several more 'ratchets', all working to keep the flow going in the right direction. The first one **a** on the valve is about 0.75 to 1mm deep, with the underhead radius blended back to suit (this mod can under some circumstances slightly reduce the flow in the right direction). This I must admit is really a job for a lathe mainly because the top and

Fig 22. Rather than matching the inlet manifold and port openings exactly, the joint can be exploited to form an anti-reversal trap as shown. Angle (d) should be around 6 degrees.

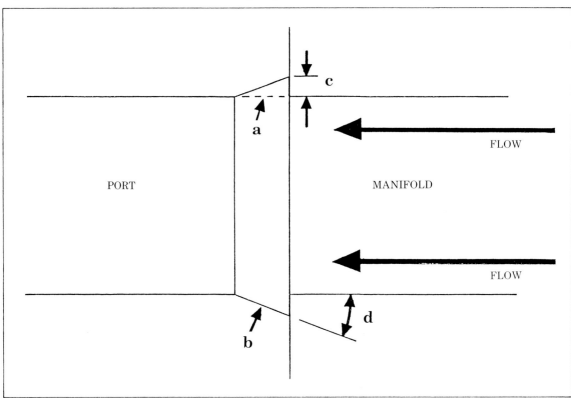

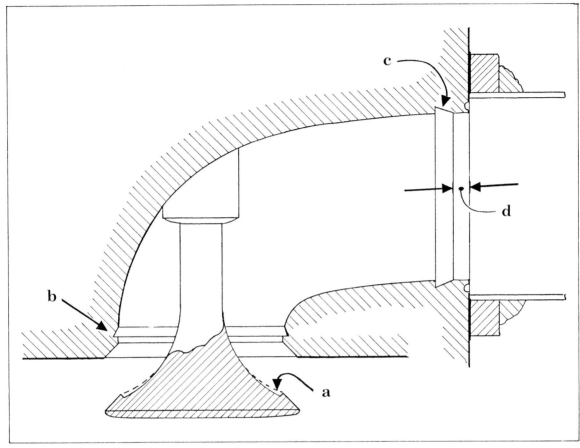

bottom edges need to be fairly sharp to be effective. Turning valves on a lathe is not as bad as it sounds; slow speeds, sharp tools, light cuts and the right lubrication are all that is required. Don't forget as it's the exhaust valve a high polish is not out of place.

Next, another 'ratchet' at **b** about 3 to 4mm behind the exhaust seat; here you are going to have to use your discretion on how deep you go for mechanical reasons, 2mm being ideal. If you are in any doubt only go in 1mm. In either case an angle of 25 degrees is about right. If you have valve seat inserts then behind these is the obvious place to form the flat face. To cut these, use a tapered rotary file in an electric drill, but be careful – one slip and all is lost once you are working on the real head.

Now on to **c** and yet another 'ratchet' but this time bigger. Leave at least 5 to 6mm at **d** from the face to the beginning of the taper, make the angle around 25 degrees and cut in about 2 to 3mm. To cut this, use a reversed taper rotary file with

Fig 23. Exhaust port in section, with anti-reversal 'ratchets' on the back of the valve (a), behind the valve seat (b) and near the manifold face (c).

65

Fig 24. A reversed taper rotary file spaced out from the electric drill chuck with washers is used for cutting 'ratchets' in the ports.

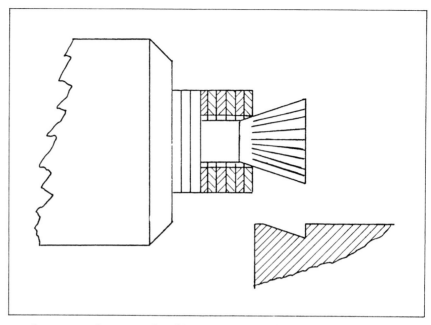

washers spacing out the distance, see **Fig 24**.

This is about as far as you can go on the model, the rest really needs to be done using metal. However, I will carry on the explanations so that you know where to come back to. So for the moment we will jump forward and assume the real cylinder head has been brought up to the same standard as the model.

Before you start again, a word or two about exhaust manifolds. If you can obtain a multibranch welded tubular one with a big bore then you are in luck. For a road car the 4-2-1 arrangement is the best as it gives you more mid-range torque. If on the other hand you are going to use the original manifold then do the same mods recommended for a small-bore tubular manifold. However, before making any mods at all there is one little job to do. That involves ensuring that whenever you replace the manifold it goes back on in exactly the same position every time, and it applies to the inlet manifold as well.

Clean the mating surfaces on both the manifold and head, then coat the manifold face lightly with engineer's blue (not marking blue). Carefully mount the manifold on to its studs or bolts making sure that the mating surfaces don't touch. Then push the manifold down to its lowest position on its threads and nip up the nuts or bolts (**Fig 25**). Now remove the manifold, and from the blue that has transferred to the head you can see how head and manifold line up. Bearing in mind the anti-reversal cuts you will be making, it should now be possible to figure out the best position for the manifold. Now clean off the

66

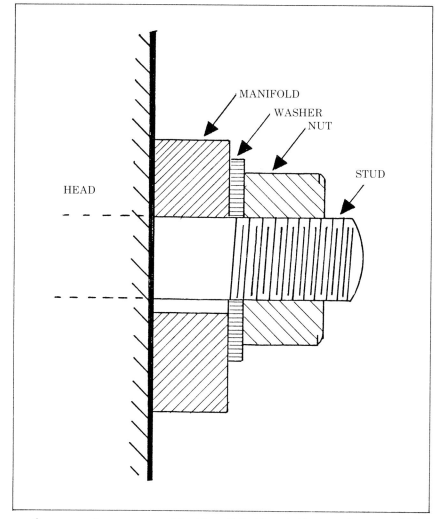

Fig 25. Exhaust manifold attachment. While the nut and washer secure the manifold flange to the head, the stud does not usually provide completely accurate location so that some variation in position is possible each time the manifold is refitted unless an additional means of alignment is provided.

MANIFOLD

WASHER

NUT

STUD

HEAD

surfaces again, reassemble (dry this time), lining the manifold up in the best position, and tighten up the nuts.

Now in an accessible place, preferably at each end of the manifold, drill two 2mm holes through the manifold and into the head; they only need to go into the head about 2mm. These now become jigging holes – any time you replace the manifold all you need to do is insert two 2mm drill shanks through the manifold and into the head, then tighten up and you will duplicate the original position. The drills shouldn't jam in the holes as they normally cut slightly oversize. Incidentally, don't forget your gaskets will probably need these holes also.

Now, at last, back to the exhaust port face and manifold. Refer to **26 A**, **B** and **C** which represent big bore, normal bore and standard cast-iron manifolds respectively. To start with, a

Fig 26. The manifold to head joint with three different types of exhaust manifold, showing how an anti-reversal trap can be provided in each case. (A) big bore fabricated manifold: (B) normal bore fabricated manifold: (C) cast manifold.

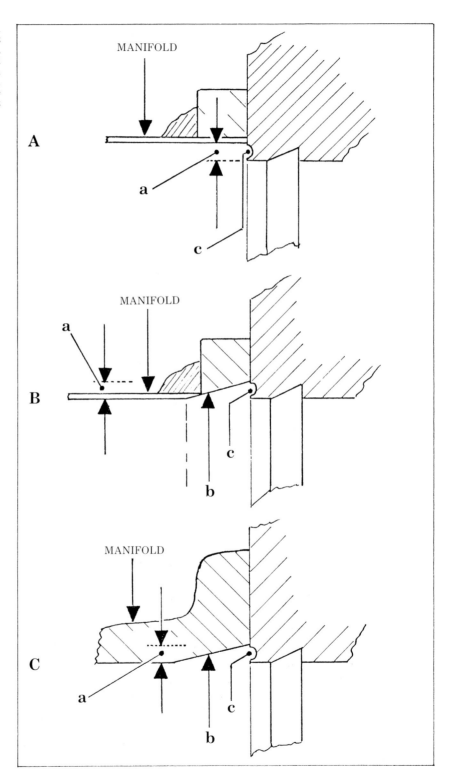

Rear view of modified inlet and exhaust valves, the former with narrowed seat, the latter with an anti-reversal 'ratchet' cut into the back of the head.

dimension at **a** of at least 3mm is required (more if possible). If you have a big bore manifold you may already have this, if not read on.

What you need is another cut as at **b**, making another 'ratchet'. This is easily done with a half round file, aiming for at least 3mm at **a** as already mentioned. The standard manifold shouldn't be any problem but be careful on the standard-bore tubular type that you don't cut through the plate and into the weld or it will fall to pieces. Keep the angle here as shallow as possible.

If you have managed to get more than 3mm at **a**, you should be able to produce a semi-circular groove all around the port as at **c**. This will give you an excellent anti-reversal port. But it is a fairly difficult thing to produce especially as it needs to be reasonably accurate. It should be about 3mm wide (1.5mm radius), leaving a distance of 1mm from the port edge and another 1mm at the outer edge. A dental burr used around a template is probably the best way of achieving this, short of having it done on a milling machine.

Before leaving anti-reversal it might be interesting to point out that it's quite simple with some head designs to use half the cylinder head model and two half valves covered with a sheet of Perspex to study flow in both directions by blowing smoke through. This works quite well at very slow speeds but don't forget the boundary layer effect on the Perspex which tends to distort things if you try and speed up too much.

7

Cutting metal

Working on the plaster model of the cylinder head is quicker and easier than working in metal, and allows plenty of scope for experiment, but you have to bear in mind that everything you do will have to be repeated later in metal if it is to be of any benefit. Once the model is developed to your satisfaction, which may mean returning to it several times after working on other components, the real cylinder head has to be brought up to the same standard. Copying all the modifications you have developed, keeping all those subtle contours and carefully tested curves and checking each dimension and shape step by step as you go, is an operation where there is no substitute for care and patience.

In practical terms, we have now reached the stage (assuming that you have already taken account of the later information on combustion chambers and compression ratios) where the next step is to transfer everything you have learnt and tried on the model to the real cylinder head. I will make no bones about it, it really is hard work: there will be times when you will doubt your sanity and seriously think about giving it all up and taking up mountain climbing or ski-jumping. But having learnt so much, don't give up now, keep at it steadily and you will eventually get there. At least (unlike me when I first started) you will know where you are going.

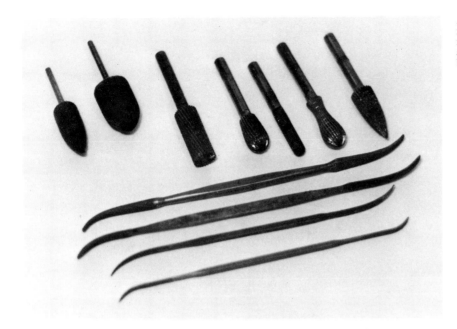

A selection of tools used in modifying a cylinder head: rotary files in various shapes above and curved riffler files below.

To measure with, you will need your vernier caliper, a pair of small ball-ended internal spring calipers and a depth gauge, at least: in fact anything that is useful can be employed. Some shapes are best transferred using templates made from styrene sheet or sausage-shaped lumps of Plasticine pressed into the shape to be copied.

To cut metal with, you will require a selection of rotary files and small grindstones to be used with an electric drill and flexible drive. Flap wheels can be useful if you find them small enough, and a length of dowel with a slot cut in the end and production paper wrapped round is handy too. Also hand files of various shapes and sizes including curved rifflers: these can be bought in sets from good tool stockists.

Don't forget when using rotary equipment to observe the safety rules and wear a mask and safety goggles. If you are tempted to think, 'I won't bother this time,' stop and consider the value of good health and unimpaired eyesight.

As it's a long and somewhat laborious job it's best to do it in short stages. I suggest doing No 1 inlet port up to a semi-finished condition, then start on No 2, then back to the first for a while. Then start on No 3. Then No 1 followed by No 2 and No 3 and then start on No 4 and so on. If you try and finish everything on one cylinder position at a time, before you get to the last you will want to give up. If you start the exhaust ports in the reverse order then you can finish everything more or less at the same time.

71

Fig 27. A template made of thin plastic or even strong card is useful in ensuring that the combustion chambers are all modified to exactly the same shape. Two holes coinciding with the valve guides enable it to be positioned accurately by inserting two valve stems or suitable pieces of rod. If the combustion chambers are arranged in handed pairs the template can be reversed to produce the mirror-image shape for the adjacent chamber.

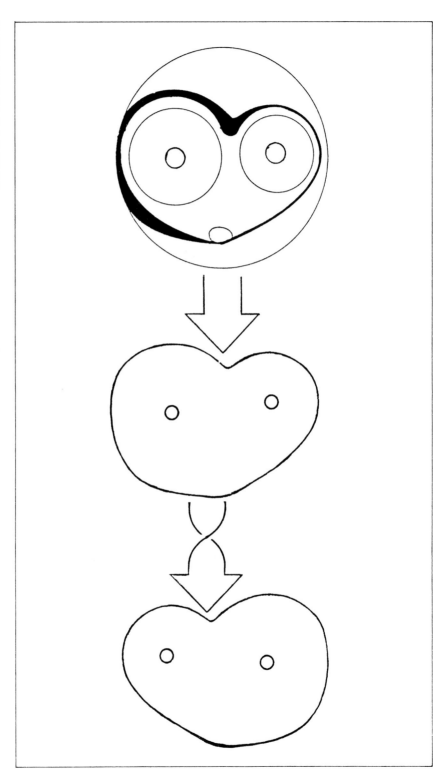

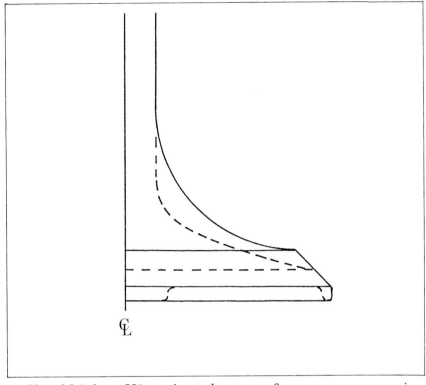

Fig 28. Profile of inlet valve with modified shape shown dotted.

C̵L

(Should it be a V8 you've taken on, of course, you are going to need twice the fortitude – but think of the end result!)

Before opening up the inlet port throat, give the valve a quick lap with fine grinding paste so you can see exactly where the seat is as a guide.

When you have finished the ports turn your attention to the valves. If you give the inlet valve a quick lap again it will show you exactly where the new narrow seat is on the valve. Start your shaping from the very edge of the seat (**Fig 28**).

When you think you have done it all, compare the flow rates under all conditions with the model. Everything should match: if it doesn't, probe and find out why and rectify. Also don't forget to make sure that all cylinders flow the same rate. Sometimes because of handed combustion chambers and different port offsets it's not quite as easy as it sounds.

That's enough physical work for the moment, so we will now go back to the grey matter and the flow rig. There are still quite a few things that require attention and we will work through them in a logical order. If the order doesn't make sense immediately, believe me there is some logic behind explaining it this way, even if you will eventually carry out the jobs in a different sequence.

Three views of a Ford 2-litre cylinder head, the inlet port on the right having been modified while that on the left is still untouched. Changes in lighting emphasize different aspects of modification in each picture. Note the rough, ridged finish of the unmodified port.

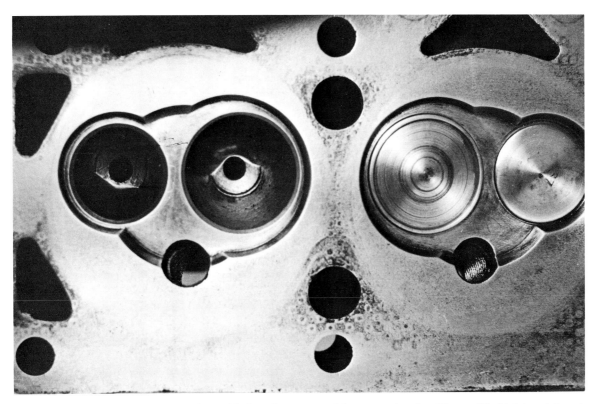

Ford 1600 crossflow head after attention, with the valves removed from one chamber. The modified inlet port throat, narrow valve seat and improved guide shape can be seen. The exhaust port similarly has the guide boss blended in and a slightly narrowed valve seat.

8

Inlet air

While we have paid a lot of attention to the inlet port in the cylinder head, and rightly so, because it is a crucial area in improving the performance of many engines, it is not the first potential obstacle to gas flow. The rest of the induction system, air cleaner, carburettor throat and manifold, needs to be examined as well, the degree of improvement that is possible varying a good deal from one design to another. Petrol bills notwithstanding, it is principally air which the engine consumes, so the quality, particularly the temperature, and quantity of the supply available to the intake is an important consideration.

As you already know, cold air is denser and therefore heavier than hot air and, whilst admitting that air being drawn into the engine is going to pick up heat from the carburettor, manifold and ports, it's fairly obvious that if the temperature of the gas when it actually reaches the cylinder can be reduced by only 5 degrees centigrade, then there is going to be more potential power. Don't forget that the fuel air ratio is measured by weight not volume, therefore cooler air can contain more fuel (until you reach the dew point but that doesn't really concern us at the moment). When you consider that most engines run at about 80 degrees centigrade and that, even when the car is moving, the under-bonnet temperature is not much below that, it's not difficult to see that if you can introduce air into the inlet at ambient temperature, the charge temperature will be considerably cooler. So if you can arrange for some way of getting cold air into the carburettor then you will gain power.

I have just come across some old notes of mine concerning the weight of air at different temperatures. At 15 degrees centigrade one cubic foot of air weighs 0.076lb, whereas at 80 degrees centigrade it only weighs 0.0625lb. If you work out how many cubic feet of air your engine consumes at its maximum then multiply by both the above figures you will be able to see beyond any doubt why cold inlet air helps to produce power.

There are two points, however, to bear in mind. The first you have probably already thought of and concerns winter driving. Some carburettors are particularly prone to icing during cold weather, because of the sudden drop in pressure and therefore temperature in the venturi or butterfly area, usually at relatively low throttle openings. If carburettor icing does happen to you or you suspect it might, arrange for an alternative air pick-up point for use in very cold weather. Most cars now have a summer/winter inlet pipe which should give you some inspiration. One idea I used is shown **Fig 29**: it's basically a slot in the bonnet with a hinged flap to shut off outside air flow if needed. It's best to put a shroud around the back and sides as shown, otherwise you won't really be drawing in cold air. Cars vary greatly when it comes to carburettor icing. One I had no problems with even in what was supposed to be the coldest weather this century, but another was an absolute pig whenever the outside temperature dropped down near zero and behaved like a 2½-cylinder kangaroo until I figured out what the problem was.

Fig 29. On some cars it may be possible to provide a fresh air feed to the air cleaner which can be closed with a flap when the outside temperature is low enough to cause carburettor icing.

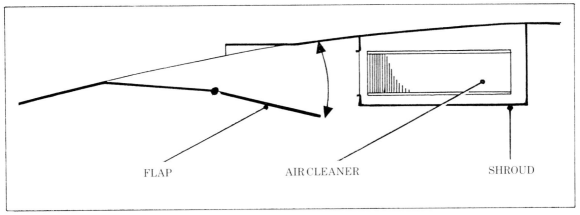

FLAP   AIR CLEANER   SHROUD

The next point about air temperature involves the manifold rather than the intake but it's convenient to talk about it here. A lot of cars have water-heated inlet manifolds or hot spots, and you could be tempted to disconnect or isolate them in pursuit of the cold inlet charge theory. But my advice is, unless your engine is for racing only, don't. I will try and explain why. The main reason for heating the charge is that at low throttle openings there is a dramatic drop in gas speed after the venturi and butterfly with a consequent tendency for the mixture to separate and it can actually form droplets of petrol on the manifold floor in bad cases. This is not a good idea: it causes, among other things, pollution, poor power production, high fuel consumption and rapid bore wear. Now if the amount of heat supplied is correct and in the right place it will warm up the mixture just sufficiently to keep it vaporized at low speeds (and so actually improve low-speed fuel consumption). However, as soon as you open the throttle the engine speeds up and the gas flow increases which rapidly cools the hot spot to the point where its effect is negligible. There will obviously be a very small increase in inlet temperature but at high gas speeds for all intents and purposes you can ignore it, because the engine is consuming air very quickly. Obviously, as usual, the full story is a bit more complicated than that and involves boundary layer and centre line temperature and flow, but that's the basics anyway.

Exhaust-heated inlet manifolds are now almost a thing of the past which is just as well, because I never met one that was any good. Basically, the problem was that when you wanted the heat to go away (when accelerating or at high speeds), that was just when they supplied the most.

Air cleaner
You should have been able to establish during your initial flow checking whether the air cleaner was a major restriction. It might not have been then, but it's worth checking again before you assemble anything, as it might well be troublesome now since you will have improved everything else. If it is now a restriction, you will have to invest in a better version. There are a few well known names on the market that are very good if you follow the instructions carefully. But some of the old pancake filters actually restrict flow more than standard units so, if you can, test before you buy. Of course, if you are prepared for the engine bores to wear out faster, just a fine gauze to keep out leaves and tram tickets will give you the best flow, but that is up to you. Most production air cleaners do a pretty good

silencing job too, so you are likely to have a significantly higher level of engine noise to live with as well as the wear problem. Whatever you do to improve the flow through the air cleaner will to some extent upset the carburettor mixture adjustment at all speeds; this is the first argument for having your final setting-up done on a rolling road.

Carburettor

It may seem that once you have established the carburettor or carburettors you are going to use or already have, there is nothing more you can do, but this is far from the truth. Most carburettors can with a little gentle persuasion be provoked

Fig 30. Box on which the carburettor can be mounted for flow testing. Opening (a) should be slightly larger than the carburettor outlet. Draught excluder (b) can be used to seal the carburettor to the box and locating blocks (c) will hold it in place. Width (d) may be limited by throttle linkage. Vacuum gauge connection (e) should be positioned out of the direct air flow.

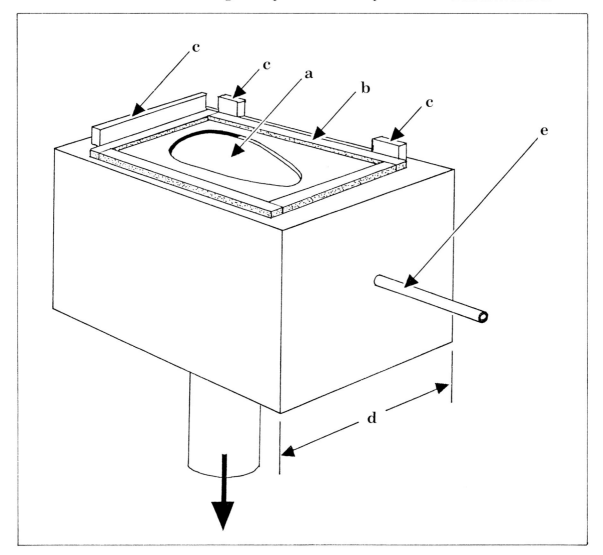

into flowing quite a bit more air – as usual, some are more easily improved than others. Obviously, as there is a great deal of variation in carburettors, this will be a general discusssion rather than a specific blow by blow account of how to do it. There are traditional methods of improvement such as streamlining the butterfly valve and shaft, and other ways which will require the use of your flow rig and probe.

The first thing you need to do is make a box to act as a plenum chamber on which you can mount your carburettor for testing, something like **Fig 30**. Make the opening **a** in the top about 3mm bigger all round than the outlet size of the carburettor (the one shown is for a compound-venturi Weber so is oval). If you are using twin choke side-draught carburettors, such as Weber DCOE or similar, then it's best to work on one choke at a time. Strips of self-adhesive draught excluder fitted round the opening will seal the face so you don't have to bolt the carburettor down every time you test it. Two locating blocks, **c**, will enable you to replace it in exactly the same position every time. The box ideally needs to be at least the same capacity as one cylinder, but the width at **d** will probably be restricted because of various levers and linkages on the butterfly shafts. The vacuum gauge pickup pipe needs to be in an area of relatively stable air and definitely out of the direct flow: I suggest you fit it in a position such as that shown at **e**.

Obviously the first thing to do is a flow check with the carburettor in perfectly standard condition. As before, the butterfly or butterflies should be locked fully open and also **make absolutely sure there is no petrol inside**. Having established your base line and noted it, it's time to start on modifications.

Firstly, as it is not a new idea, we will start on the butterfly valve and spindle. By making the upstream side of the valve into a knife edge you will improve things slightly, though this will probably only be measurable with the manometer at an angle (beware of water in the motor). The idea is to take metal off only the non-critical side of the valve (**Fig 31**); make sure before you do this that it will not interfere with the opening or closing of any balance or bleed holes in the carburettor wall. Forget the trailing edge of the valve, you can't do anything to it that will improve things to any extent.

The spindle can be modified to effect quite a useful gain in flow. There are usually two enormous screwheads sticking out into the flow (**Fig 32A**); these can either be reduced in size or replaced with countersunk-head screws. The spindle itself can be modified by filing flat as shown in **Fig 32B**. Flat is better

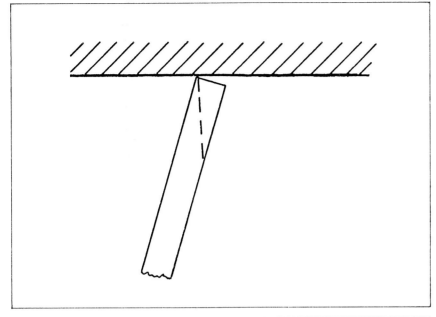

Fig 31. To improve air flow through the carburettor, the leading edge of the throttle butterfly can be thinned down. Metal should be removed only from the non-critical side so that the sealing of the butterfly against the carburettor wall is not impaired.

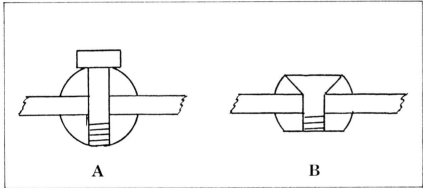

A   B

Fig 32. The attachment of the throttle butterfly to the spindle is often by protruding screws (A). Flattening the spindle (taking care not to weaken it unduly) and using countersunk screws (B) will reduce the obstruction.

than streamlined in this case for two reasons. Firstly, if you try and streamline it you will probably finish up by making it too weak and secondly, the mixture has already been separated by the leading edge of the butterfly valve so it's really the smallest cross-sectional area you are after. By all means experiment and prove me wrong, but my best flows have been achieved with the spindle thinned down to about the same thickness on each side as the butterfly valve itself and then secured by countersunk screws.

If your carburettor has interchangeable venturis then you could go up in size but, as this usually requires complete recalibration, it can be expensive. On other carburettors, if you are careful, you can open up the venturi yourself, but for obvious reasons this tends to be rather risky as it is only too easy to upset the flow completely and ruin the carburettor. What I usually do is to take some light cuts around the venturi with a model maker's half-round file over as much of the surface as possible. Then, using progressively finer grades of wet and dry paper, polish out the scratch marks, trying to keep to the original contour. Final smoothing is with Scotch Brite and metal polish, this being one of the few places where a polished finish *can* help, as it is the area of highest gas speed and therefore the boundary layer is very thin. SU carburettors and the like are best just polished in this area unless you are prepared to experiment for hours, so if you decide the carburettor is a limitation it's probably quicker and cheaper in the long run to pick up the next bigger size from a car breakers.

Next, heading out towards the inlet, comes the choke plate or butterfly. You can throw it and its shaft away, as long as your carburettor has an accelerator pump. Fill the holes that are left with Araldite, and sand and polish back to match the inlet shape. To start the engine in cold weather, a few pumps on the pedal will prime it, then the high idle speed part of the choke mechanism will keep it running – it's obviously best if you can warm the engine for a few minutes before driving away, to avoid stalling. Incidentally, if you have an automatic choke, throw it as far away as you can. Removing the choke plate will improve the flow just a little bit more, every little helps. (If your carburettor has a different sort of cold-start device you don't need to worry as it won't hinder the flow anyway.)

Now on to the carburettor intake. On normally aspirated racing engines the inlet usually starts with a trumpet so this is obviously a good thing to aim for. If you have the space, funds and the right type of carburettor, there are some good quality trumpets with matching filters on the market. There are, though, also some cheap and nasty trumpets around which might look good to the uninitiated. They can usually be improved by testing with your probe and rectifying as required. If you don't have a carburettor that's suitable for a trumpet, it is still possible to improve the flow, and the way of doing this is much the same as for improving a badly designed trumpet, so I will explain what to aim for in either case.

From the relatively stationary outside air to the beginning of the venturi in the carburettor, the air speed and pressure should ideally change gradually with no sudden jumps in either. To achieve this ideal completely, the trumpets would need to be so large that they wouldn't fit under the bonnet. So a compromise is made that causes the flow at the outer edge to

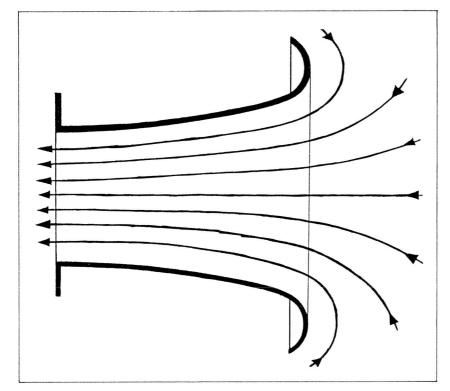

Fig 33. A properly designed
carburettor intake trumpet
gathers air from a wider area
than the choke diameter and
channels it smoothly in without inducing flow-limiting
turbulence.

roll around the lip so that air is sucked in from behind as well
as in front; study the streamlines in **Fig 33** to get the idea. This
can be very nearly as efficient at maximum flow as the
theoretically correct shape, and for lower flow rates can
actually be even more effective.

To put all this into practice, set your carburettor up on the
flow box, then run your probe from a point just in front of the
venturi up the side to the upper lip and around it. You will
probably be surprised how far round the lip the flow is
measurable. If your carburettor inlet is shaped as **Fig 34**, quite
a common arrangement, you will probably find that, until you
get to **a**, things are not too bad. From **a** to the lip conditions will
be constant, then confusion sets in, especially at high flow
rates. What you need to do is file out the lip to a taper, **a** in
Fig 35, then with Plasticine build up a radius all the way
round the inlet, **b**: try 6 or 7mm diameter to start with. Now try
another probe test. With any luck you will have smoothed the
air flow into the carburettor by an appreciable amount. It's
worth trying bigger radii if you have the room, going for the
biggest you can get in. When you have decided upon the size,
copy this using a flexible car body filler. If you score the outside
of the carburettor well and degrease it there shouldn't by any

83

Fig 34. Probing to check air flow in the upper or outer part of the carburettor. The flow will probably be satisfactory after point (a) but may well be less so before.

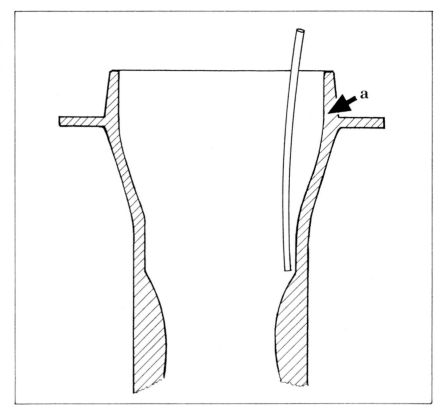

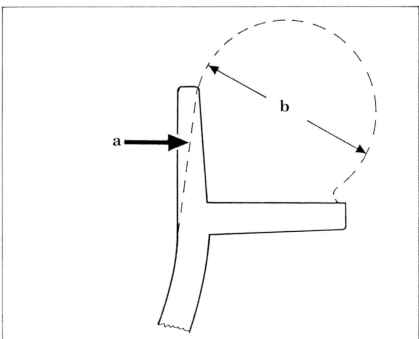

Fig 35. The carburettor intake can often be improved by tapering the outer section (a) and adding a rolled lip (b) with a diameter of 6 or 7mm.

problems with the filler coming unstuck. Because some body fillers are porous, it's best to prime and paint it once you have finished, to stop petrol getting in and causing it to soften.

Much the same procedure can be used for testing and modifying a suspect add-on trumpet or any other intake attached to the carburettor. Incidentally, if you have really effective trumpets giving good flow results, reverse pressure wave tuning won't work as the reverse pressure wave is dispersed by the trumpet. But ram tuning, which is different, does still work.

Inlet manifold
I have already explained the advantages of keeping the inlet charge cool and dealt with the question of heated inlet manifolds and hot spots. There are some non-crossflow engines where the inlet picks up too much heat simply because of its proximity to the exhaust manifold. So if your manifolds are close, it's an idea to try and fit a shield between them and perhaps arrange for a supply of rammed cold air between the shield and exhaust. This won't help the soak temperature at standstill or slow speeds but will be of benefit when you are travelling at normal speeds.

The first step with the inlet manifold itself is obviously flow testing. Manufacturers these days have at long last just about got things right, at least as far as mixture distribution is concerned. They have had to make improvements for at least two reasons, the advent of compound carburettors and the stricter anti-pollution laws in many markets. That doesn't mean that there is nothing to do, however. If you can run a flexibly mounted flap wheel up through the tracts it will clean up any excess casting roughness and help to increase flow. Also look out for any sharp edges that might be obstructing or slowing the flow. If you use your flow rig, experimenting with both the Plasticine ball and the probe technique, you will be able to identify any major problems in need of rectification. If you have to compromise between total flow and balanced distribution, choose the latter every time as it's vital that all the cylinders are *equally* well fed.

If you are after maximum power at all costs then it remains true that, exotic fuel-injection systems aside, one carburettor choke per cylinder is the only way to go. But before you commit yourself to that sort of expense, try everything else recommended and I think you will be pleasantly surprised. To quote a specific example, a Ford 1600 GT engine (the early semi-chambered crossflow version), with a Piper 285 cam,

4-2-1 Demon Tweeks exhaust manifold, 10.4 to 1 compression ratio, the standard DFM Weber carburettor and normal inlet manifold, had the head, ports, valves and so on modified as outlined in this book. It produced a verified 125bhp at the flywheel and 105lb/ft of torque – very exciting in a Mk1 Escort Sport! One friend was convinced I had managed somehow to fit secret Nitrous Oxide injection and he searched fruitlessly for ages. It would also run at 20mph in top gear and pull away cleanly, demonstrating better than standard tractability.

Before we leave inlet manifolds, a quick word about aftermarket ones. There are a few well known names who make good ones but unfortunately there are also some that are absolute rubbish and seem to have been designed for the foundryman's benefit rather than for gas flow. I came across one that looked very pretty, with polished ribs on it, but actually flowed less (and with worse distribution) than a bog-standard non-GT version for the same engine. How do you choose? I don't know the answer to this: either keep your eyes open and see what the successful people are using (not the posers), or, like me, lose some money learning the hard way. If in any doubt, stick to the manufacturers' original rather than take the risk.

9

Exhaust system

Looking at ways of encouraging gas flow in the right direction through the engine has already led us to consider the first part of the exhaust system, the junction of the head and manifold. Now we must examine the rest of the system, both the manifold itself and the subsequent pipework, including silencers, which conduct the gases back to the atmosphere. A beautifully free-flowing intake and cylinder head are of no avail if there are severe restrictions further down the line. Practical constraints imposed on the length and shape of the system by its location under the vehicle, as well as the need to limit noise, mean that a degree of compromise is inevitable on any road car.

Having just condemned a lot of aftermarket inlet manifolds I will make up for it by saying that most aftermarket exhaust manifolds work well. The only things to watch out for really are the quality of the welding and the alignment on the port face.

Pressure wave extraction at the resonant frequencies still works with the anti-reversal ports but at a slightly higher engine speed due to the effectively shortened length of the pipes. This is another reason why I recommend 4-2-1 manifolds rather than 4-1 types as the latter might take the extraction effect above your rev limit.

There's not much more to say about tubular manifolds. By all means flow check them by sucking through the outlet pipe with all the ports blocked off in turn except the one being tested. If you do find anything seriously wrong, there's not a lot you can do, due to the thinness of the material, unless it's something obvious like a blob of weld in the way. While it might be nice to tailor-make a manifold to match your engine exctly, that's really outside the scope of this book, requiring specialized knowledge and equipment.

If you are using a standard cast-iron manifold it may well be possible by probing one tract at a time to achieve quite a good flow increase. Just cleaning up the casting roughness usually improves things a bit. Use a flexibly mounted flap wheel, and finish matt not polished as we want the manifold to start dissipating heat, not contain it. Already the gas is cooling and will start to deposit carbon which unfortunately acts as a heat barrier. As on other parts, aim for a balanced flow, using the now well rehearsed means. The exhaust (within limits) is not quite as critical as the inlet side.

Exhaust system
Before we even start on the exhaust I have to get rid of a misconception that, despite being proved wrong by numerous far more knowledgeable people than myself, still lingers on, the idea that some restriction in the exhaust system is somehow necessary. So let's be quite clear: any back pressure in the exhaust system costs power and petrol. I think the misconception might have started when someone fitted a free-flowing exhaust without altering anything else and quite naturally the car didn't run as well as before, and it snowballed from there. I have met people who have indeed done just that and when asked if they had rejetted or readjusted the carburettor, said 'no', looked vague and asked why they needed to. I think you probably know the answer to that anyway.

Think for the moment of the engine complete with the inlet and exhaust system as a means of pumping air, as opposed to compressing it. Now with the exhaust outlet blocked up, rotate the crankshaft at maximum revs and see how much air you actually pump. The answer, obviously, is none, all you will do is compress some in the exhaust. Now think of the same circumstances but with a small hole, say 2mm diameter, in the outlet: now you will pump some air but not much compared with the potential of the system and you will still be compressing it. Carrying the idea even further, if you slowly increase the size of the hole the air flow will increase and the pressure will drop, which is just what we want. Convinced? If not, stick a potato up the exhaust pipe, then try and start the engine! It won't even produce enough power to idle, will it?

Most cheap exhaust systems and some original equipment ones are made on pipe benders that actually squash the pipe slightly when it's bent. This is exactly the opposite of what it should be. Most books on mechanical engineering give you tables and formulae showing that flow through a straight pipe is far superior to one with a bend in it, assuming the same size, of course; the tighter the bend the worse the flow.

If you have to use a standard exhaust system, or parts of one, shop around and look at what is available before you buy. You are looking for a system that gives as little back pressure as possible. The way to achieve this is to use large diameter tubing with as few bends as possible. If you want to do it yourself the main problems, power-wise, that you will have to try and design around are that the system has to be silenced and usually the pipe has to be far too long.

Before you leap into the design stage, a few words on flow testing. It is possible to measure flow through a bench-mounted, fully assembled exhaust system but due to its physical size and the small readings you will get on your manometer it's not a single-handed job. The next problem with doing the whole system at once is that it requires a lot of holes to be drilled in the pipes and silencers, ideally with a manometer attached to each one. You have to find a satisfactory and permanent way of sealing them afterwards and that's not as easy as it sounds.

Bearing that in mind, I think the best compromise is to do the flow testing one section at a time, adding short lengths of pipe or tube at each end with reading holes, and sucking in each direction to establish the best way round. By now you will have a pretty good idea of what to look for. So let's go through the exhaust from front to back: while each case will be different in detail, the basic advice is widely applicable.

About 90 to 100 centimetres back from the manifold face if you are using a standard manifold, or at the end of a multi-branch manifold, you ideally need an expansion chamber. This serves several purposes; it allows the gas to start cooling, it imparts a small amount of silencing and, if it's properly designed, can serve as the end of the tuned length of the exhaust pipe. Expansion chambers come in several types, some are plain chambers, others have a silencer in the second half. I think the plain chamber is better, preferring to start the silencing with cooler gas further back if possible. A cross

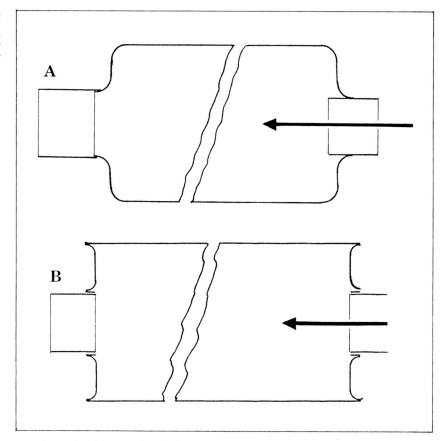

section of what to look for is shown in **Fig 36**, **A** being a good design and **B** being a bad one. Ideally the expansion chamber should have at least the same volume as the engine.

After the expansion chamber, a length of straight pipe is needed. I know the problems, but make this as long as possible, with the first silencer just in front of the rear wheels followed by a nice gentle curve over the rear axle or whatever happens to be in the way, then into the rear silencer and out of the tail pipe.

All pipe joints should assist the flow, always going from a smaller diameter to a larger one, and this includes exits from the expansion chamber and silencers. With a lot of standard exhausts, the pipe diameter gradually reduces at each stage. I know the *theory* is that the gas is cooling and contracting but I believe in fact it's done for cheapness, and I recommend you do the opposite. Incidentally, if you look at cars fitted with turbos you will find the exhaust is usually enormous compared to the standard, non-turbo one as any back pressure would inhibit the turbine's rotation. The exception (and there always is one) is where the exhaust size is used as a boost limiter.

It would be very difficult indeed, and take a great deal of time, to assess and understand all the possible variables relating to silencers. If possible, I use two of the straight-through absorbtion pattern of the best quality I can afford (sometimes that has meant from the scrapyard, but that really is a false economy). In practical terms, an element of compromise, taking into account what's available and what will fit under the car in question, is inevitable. There is, though, no need to have a noisy exhaust – it is unsocial, unnecessary and can actually stop you using your hard-won performance at times. When you consider all the things that rob your engine of power, the silencers usually come a long way down the list.

I don't usually like to quote specific brands but clearly Janspeed have a very good reputation in this field and do make a wide range of systems. If they do one for your car and you can afford it, it could well be the best bet.

Before we leave exhausts, perhaps I should mention the fashion which seems to come back every few years for gadgets you can fix on to the tailpipe which are claimed to help extraction. I haven't found one yet that works. If you think about it, the exhaust gas speed will always be higher than the forward speed of the car. Even if you could design an extractor venturi that would work in the turbulent region under the rear of a car, it would be so big that it would slow the car down due to air drag.

10

Combustion chamber

Raising the compression ratio is a sure way of increasing the power of an engine, but in practical terms there are limiting factors. It is important to distinguish between the theoretical and effective compression ratios, and the valve timing must be taken into account here. Checking the combustion chamber volume is part of the calculation. First, though, it is worth pointing out some subtle ways in which the shape of the combustion chamber can influence the flow patterns. With some engines this is another possible area for improvement.

Although this chapter might at first seem to be in the wrong place it isn't – don't forget I did ask you to read right through the book before starting any work. Now that you have made yourself a nice cylinder head and valves with everything else gas flowed to suit, it's time to look at some rather more obscure flow helpers and hinderers.

The first of the hinderers is already fairly well known. On some engines the inlet port directs the incoming gas straight at the cylinder wall, causing a number of unfortunate side-effects apart from slowing down the gas (**Fig 37 A**). This is usually overcome, as a by-product of creating swirl in the cylinder, by offsetting the port (**Fig 37 B**). Swirl as opposed to turbulence helps promote even and more complete combustion, which can allow higher compression ratios.

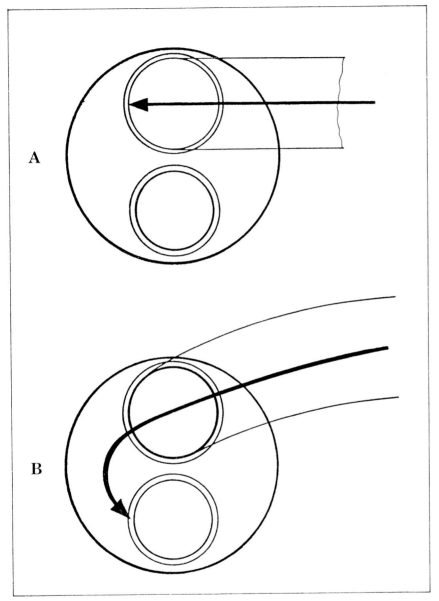

A

B

If your engine is suspect in this respect or has no port offset it's worth doing a test on your model with a transparent dummy cylinder made out of rolled clear acetate sheet. By sucking smoke through you can actually see what happens; do this at different flow rates for a complete picture.

Now, bearing the next section in mind, you can start your experiments. If you remember, we produced a venturi on the far side of the port wall to help us hold the flow on the inner radius. Rotate this idea by 90 degrees on to the other axis and

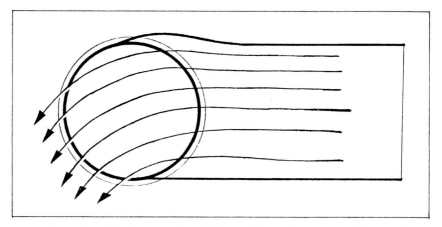

Fig 38. A degree of swirl can be induced in a basically straight port by curving one side to create a venturi effect.

experiment with it: you should be able to improve things. Just remember to try and complement any swirl that's already there or that you have built in for other reasons. **Fig 38** should make the idea clear enough.

On bath tub or similar shaped combustion chambers another hinderer can be the shape of the chamber itself, because it tends to mask both of the valves round part of their circumference, see the shaded areas in **Fig 39**. This obviously becomes more critical with higher valve lifts. Because the flow is outwards, the exhaust is not restricted as much as the inlet. It's quite simple with a ruler, paper and pencil to work out if you have any masking taking place, especially at full lift. But don't forget that no matter what you have done the highest percentage of gas is still flowing over the far side of the valve and that the area at **a** is the really critical dimension. If you have built-in swirl already or have added it yourself it will tend to move the critical area to a slightly better position nearer to the centre line. However, carve some plaster away on

Fig 39A. Shaded areas indicated how combustion chambers of bath tub shape can sometimes mask the valve opening area. In opening the chamber out to reduce this effect it is of course essential not to go beyond the line of the cylinder wall.

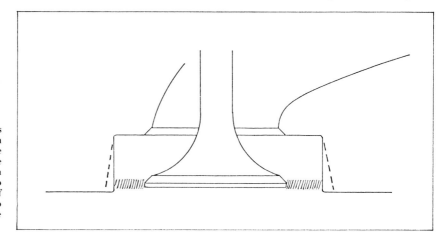

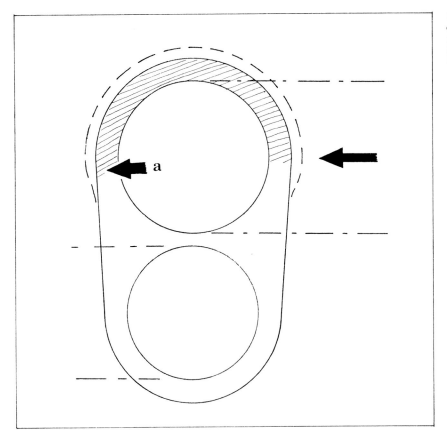

Fig 39B. Bath tub combustion chamber in plan view. Masking effect is most critical at (a) opposite the inlet port.

the model as shown by the dotted line and see if you can improve things: bear in mind, though, that this could help *or* hinder the swirl pattern.

Now on to the related subject of helpers. If you study **Fig 40 A** and **B**, which show the same combustion chamber and valve at different lifts, you will see that it acts as a system of venturis with really no sudden changes of section (which as you know

Fig 40. Detail of inlet valve and combustion chamber at different valve lifts, showing how an opening with no abrupt changes of section maintains boundary flow and avoids turbulence.

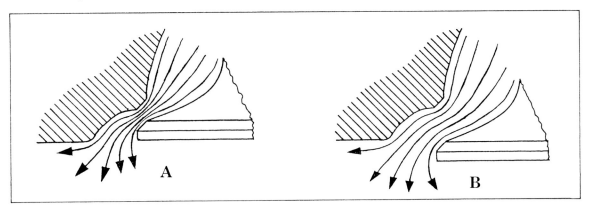

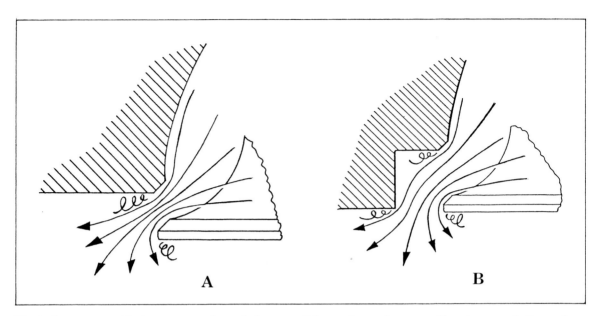

A   B

Fig 41. In contrast with the previous illustration, these shapes break up the flow round the edge of the inlet valve and so introduce turbulence and resistance.

cause breakdown of boundary layer adhesion and therefore turbulence). Compare this with **Fig 41 A** and, even worse, **B** and you will see the sudden changes that occur in this second case. Valves with modified rims help a little here in all cases. If you test with a thin probe and a clear cylinder (mainly to let you see where you are), using an angled manometer, it is possible to prove this effect for yourself. To improve things, however, is rather more difficult. In fact on flat-faced heads (curses on them for other reasons as well) there's really nothing you can do. On other heads the previous mod if done with this in mind also can help. Pinto heads respond fairly well, and so do the early crossflow Ford heads, the ones with combustion chambers about 3mm deep (in fact I have made small-valve versions flow more than big-valve flat-head versions). Bath tub and similar shapes can be improved as long as you bear everything else in mind. The hemispherical head, perhaps purely by accident, does quite well in this department which is just as well because there's not much you could do about it.

Just before we leave the combustion chambers and ports, another flow test to try is with the valves both open and the piston at TDC to see how much of the incoming inlet gas gets directed straight out of the exhaust valve. All other things being equal, if you have developed everything as so far outlined, then it shouldn't be a big problem and if it is then by now you should have a pretty good idea on how to effect a cure, although some of the things we have already done should help.

96

If you decide to incorporate any of these mods, do so before you proceed to the next section but not before you have read through the rest of the book.

Compression ratio

One sure and undisputed way to increase the volumetric efficiency and therefore power of an engine is by increasing its pressure ratio, which means either turbocharging, super-charging or, in our case, increasing compression ratio. Now like just about everything else to do with engines, it's not quite that simple because if you increase above a certain point detonation sets in which can wreck an engine quicker than anything. By detonation I don't mean pinking which is a relatively minor problem, I mean KNOCKING followed usually by very rapid disintegration. The problem is that no two engines (not even supposedly identical ones) have exactly the same compression ratio limit. Also, in recent years the octane rating (anti-knock or detonation limit) of petrol on sale has been getting lower all the time. With all this in mind, not to mention other problems, it's no wonder that manufacturers and tuners (myself included) tend to err on the conservative side if they want their engines to last.

Unfortunately, within the brief of this book there is no magic formula for determining the safe upper limit of the compression ratio; all I can do is tell you of a safe way to raise it that shouldn't cause you any problems. It won't contribute much to any increase of power output by itself. Having put so much work into an engine it would be a pity to spread it all over the road the first time you floor the accelerator (fortunately this time I don't speak from experience). If you wish to increase the ratio by more than the amount recommended in the following method, be it on your own head – and I don't mean the cylinder head, either!

The first thing you need to do is determine the exact theoretical compression ratio of your engine, that's if you don't already know it. This is done by taking the exact cylinder size or swept volume, adding to this the volume that it's compressed into and then dividing by the compressed size. As an example, if your swept volume for each cylinder is 400cc and your compressed volume is 42cc then the theoretical compression ration will be as follows:

$$\frac{400 + 42}{42} = \frac{442}{42} = 10.5 : 1$$

The best way to find the swept volume is by calculation, the exact bore area in square centimetres multiplied by the stroke in centimetres. Conversely, the only really practical way of finding the compressed volume is by measuring with the engine assembled (with both valves shut and the piston at TDC).

Assuming that the engine is assembled (or dry assembled if you are halfway through your mods) this is the method. First, making sure that the plug hole is vertical and the piston at TDC, fill the combustion chamber with liquid until it's about 4 or 5 threads up the plug hole (beware trapping pockets of air) and note the capacity. Any liquid can be used, preferably coloured but not too thin, like paraffin, or it will leak past the piston rings. The only really accurate way to measure the quantity is to run it into the cylinder from a burette, noting the level before and after the cylinder is full. Burettes graduated in cc can be purchased from most large chemist shops. Once you have done this, you will need a second reading with the head off to enable you to make the necessary calculations. Using Vaseline, seal a flat plate to the lower edge of the combustion chamber then fill again with liquid and take a second reading, this being the one that you will subsequently have to change by the required amount to alter the compression ratio. Depending on your engine, this will be either larger or smaller than the original reading because of the shape of the piston crown and its exact height at TDC. If your engine has combustion chambers in the pistons and a flat head then it's the piston chamber volume you have to measure.

This volume can then be used as already explained to obtain the theoretical compression ratio. Taking as an example an engine with bore and stroke of 80 x 63mm and a compression volume measured at 39cc:

Bore diameter = 80mm
so bore radius = 4cm
and bore area (using πr^2) = 50cm^2.
Stroke = 63mm = 6.3cm
so swept volume = (50 x 6.3)cc = 315cc.
Thoretical compression ratio is
$$\frac{315 + 39}{39} = \frac{354}{39} = 9.0{:}1$$

The effective ratio, however, is not quite the same as this theoretical figure, and the next step is to work out the corrected compression ratio. Because the inlet valve shuts when the piston is on it's way up the compression stroke, you will need to make an adjustment on the stroke length based on the actual closing point of the valve with the original camshaft. The best way to do this quickly is with a full scale drawing done as accurately as possible. First draw a circle (**Fig 42**) corresponding to the stroke of your engine. Mark up vertically from BDC the exact between-centres length of your connecting rod, **a**. Now around the circle make a mark the number of degrees after BDC that the valve closes with your original camshaft, **b**, for example 45 degrees. Then make a mark using the con rod length again on to the centre line at **c**. Now measure the distance between **a** and **c**, which is in this case 6mm, and subtract this from the full stroke dimension, giving the actual proportion that is compressed from the time the valve shuts. Repeat the calculation deducting the 6mm from the stroke length.

Bore area = 50cm^2
Stroke = (6.3–0.6)cm = 5.7cm
Therefore swept volume = (50 x 5.7)cc = 285cc.
Corrected compression ratio = $\dfrac{285 + 39}{39} = \dfrac{324}{39} = 8.3{:}1$

The next step is to compare that to the new proposed valve timing. So make a mark on the stroke circle at your new inlet valve closing position, say 60 degrees, **d**; then as before mark off the connecting rod length on the centre line, **e**. Measure the distance from this to the mark with the connecting rod at BDC, **a**, which in this case is 12mm, and subtract this from the stroke length to give you the new effective compression stroke. You will see that due to the geometry the extra 15 degrees makes as much difference as the original 45 degrees which is why you really have to draw the whole thing.

Bore area = 50cm^2
Stroke = (6.3–1.2)cm = 5.1cm
Therefore swept volume = (50 x 5.1)cc = 255cc.
Corrected compression ratio = $\dfrac{255 + 39}{39} = \dfrac{294}{39} = 7.5{:}1$

Two thing now begin to be clear. Firstly, what we are aiming for is to bring the corrected compression ratio back up to what it was with a standard camshaft. Secondly, if you fit a modified camshaft without raising the compression ratio the required amount you cannot be utilizing its full capabilities. This can also explain why you see some incredibly high ratios quoted for rallying and racing engines – it means that they have long-duration cams fitted so they can get away with it.

We now want to know what size compression space we need

Fig 42. Diagram used to relate inlet valve closing to piston position. As the valve closes after bottom dead centre, the piston is already travelling up the bore on the compression stroke and the distance travelled, which varies according to the valve timing determined by the camshaft profile, should be deducted from the stroke dimension when calculating the effective compression ratio.

(a) piston position at BDC. (b) valve closing point with original camshaft. (c) piston position at valve closure with original camshaft. (d) valve closing point with revised camshaft. (e) piston position at valve closure with revised camshaft. (X) stroke dimension. (Y) connecting rod length between centres.

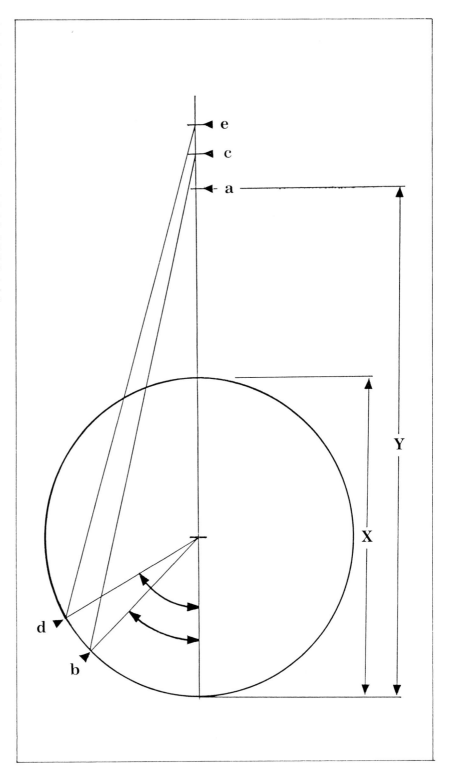

100

to raise the corrected ratio from 7.5:1 to 8.3:1. Working to the nearest whole figure, 35cc is pretty close:

$$\frac{255 + 35}{35} = \frac{290}{35} = 8.28:1$$

So 35cc is the volume you now have to aim for.

If, purely out of interest, you work out the new theoretical compression ratio, I think you might be in for a surprise:

$$\frac{315 + 35}{35} = \frac{350}{35} = 10:1$$

As you will see, it's gone up by one whole point, and I haven't been juggling with figures too much, either. The bore, stroke, con rod length and original compression ratio all come from the Ford Kent 1300 engine, and the valve timing figures are representative of camshafts fitted to that engine.

Now we know what compressed volume is required, and this can be translated into a combustion chamber volume by adding or subtracting the difference between the volumes arrived at by the two different measuring methods you used to check the engine initially, the first with the assembled engine, the second with the head removed and covered with a flat plate. Then it's just a case of finding out where to take metal from and how much. If you have the combustion chamber in the head it's reasonably straightforward. The easy way (though not the most accurate) is, with spark plug and valves fitted, to set the head on the bench with the chamber uppermost and level it as accurately as you can using a spirit level. Then pour in from the burette the exact volume you require. Using your vernier caliper as a depth gauge, very carefully measure down to the surface of the liquid; do this in at least four places and take an average. This will be the dimension that needs to be removed from the head face to change your compression ratio the desired amount. If you are using a water-based liquid a small drop of washing-up liquid will help stop it leaping up to your measuring device.

If you have a flat-faced head then you will obviously have to measure the amount into the piston crown. Then the dimension obtained has to come off the cylinder block and maybe piston, which is unfortunate as it tends to make things more expensive. Do be careful also that you are not going to run into problems with the valves hitting the pistons; 1mm is about the minimum clearance you should aim for even if it means modifying the pistons and although there is usually no difficulty in this respect, it is well worth checking. If you do have to modify the pistons, either for valve clearance or to adjust the compression ratio, be careful that the crown thickness is not reduced too drastically.

Once you have the desired amount removed from the head (or block), clean up any sharp edges and double check the capacity using the flat plate method. On some engines the only sure way is to do a dummy assembly and measure that way as well. If you have removed too much from the face, it should be possible by blending and radiusing to gain the extra capacity again. If, on the other hand, you haven't removed enough it's either back to the machine shop or accept it as it is.

Before we leave compression ratios, there are a few more points to make. Because the inlet system you have developed is more efficient than the original, at high revs you will be packing more gas into the cylinder (although your effective ratio is the same). This will bring you closer to the detonation point on your engine, and this is something you should remember before you increase beyond the corrected ratio. A phenomenon that can sometimes occur on engines with high compression ratios and wide overlap valve timing is that when switched off they run on. The answer is simple, put the car in top gear and as you switch off ease your foot off the clutch and stall it! I know it may sound brutal but if you time it right it isn't. The final word on compression ratios shouldn't really need mentioning, but I will just in case. Please make sure that the compression ratios are exactly the same for each cylinder.

11

Concluding remarks

Calculating gas speed: what to do and not to do when rebuilding the engine: competition engines: and final diversions.

I did promise earlier that I would describe a device for measuring the gas speed in your ports and inlet tracts. I know before anyone tells me that it's not perfect but as it will be used basically as a comparative instrument it should achieve what you want. The device in its simplest form consists of a U-shaped tube of about 2mm bore shaped as shown in **Fig 43**, which is then connected by flexible tubing to your manometer, the point **a** being where you are actually measuring the speed. It's easy to make, the only problem being the initial calibration. The best way to do this is to hold it in the carburettor inlet (at a place where you can measure the size easily) and then, with the engine running steadily, note the rev counter and manometer readings. Repeat for a series of different specific engine speeds. Then by some simple maths (more in a minute) you can make a conversion chart relating gas speed to manometer reading.

Now to qualify a few things: obviously the rest of the tube is causing a restriction thus giving you a false reading, but you will be taking most of the readings in roughly the same sized holes so at least it will be consistently wrong. Also to be completely accurate the other side of the manometer should be

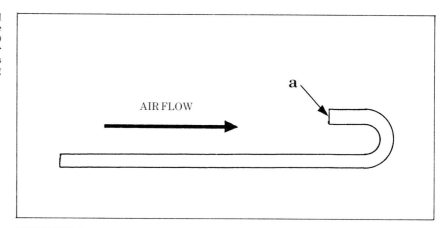

Fig 43. U-shaped probe used to measure gas speed in the inlet tract. The open end (a) is held in the carburettor intake and the other end is connected by flexible tubing to a manometer.

AIR FLOW

a

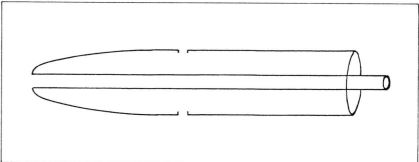

Fig 44. Theoretically ideal probe with concentric tube for simultaneous registering of static pressure at the measuring point: in practice, this refinement is hardly necessary and it greatly complicates construction as well as tending to increase the obstruction of the inlet tract and hence the danger of falsifying the reading.

connected to measure the static pressure where you are measuring the speed; this is usually done with concentric tubes, one being blocked off at the front end with side slots (**Fig 44**). This, however, tends to be even more of a restriction than the simple type as well as being far more difficult to make.

Here are the formulae for working out the mean gas speed in a known size of port or opening. You will first need to know the mean piston speed of your engine in feet per minute.

$$\text{Mean piston speed (ft/min)} = \frac{\text{rpm x stroke (in)}}{6}$$

$$\text{Mean gas velocity in port (ft/sec)} = \frac{\text{Piston speed}}{60} \times \frac{\text{D x D}}{\text{d x d}}$$

(where D = bore diameter in inches and d = port diameter in inches)

I make no apologies for using imperial measurements here. As we still use miles per hour to measure speed, it seems logical to measure gas velocity in the good old way as well.

If we take as an example an engine with bore and stroke of 82mm x 63mm (3.23in x 2.48in) running at 6,200rpm and with a port diameter of 33mm (1.3in), then –

$$\text{Mean piston speed} = \frac{6{,}200 \times 2.48}{6} = 2{,}562\text{ft/min}$$

$$\text{Gas speed in port} = \frac{2{,}562}{60} \times \frac{3.23 \times 3.23}{1.3 \times 1.3}$$

$$= 42.7 \times \frac{10.43}{1.69}$$
$$= 42.7 \times 6.17$$
$$= 263.5\text{ft/sec}$$

So the gas speed in our hypothetical port is 263.5 feet per second, which is about 180mph.

As I explained earlier, such figures are really rather academic, and I don't often measure air speed any more. What I do is to establish that my vacuum cleaner is moving air fast enough at maximum flow. If it isn't, I couple two cleaners together and use bigger bore connecting pipes.

Engine rebuilding

Although basic engine rebuilding is really outside the scope of this book and I have assumed all along that the reader can cope with the routine jobs competently, there are a few things that ought to be mentioned. Having from a very early age spent most of my life (which is far longer than I care to admit), either rebuilding or maintaining engines that people have ridden over, raced over, driven behind or in front of, raced behind or in front of, hovered in front of, flown in front of or behind (and I still do some of these), I think I can say that I have a reasonable experience of working with high performance engines (is 1500mph fast enough for high performance?). If it has taught me anything it must be that you can never be too careful when assembling an engine. I have seen the consequences of carelessness ranging from the humorous to the catastrophic. The funniest must have been the cylinder block of an old Austin Seven leaping up and down because it had come loose from the crankcase (they were detachable, by the way). The point of this, however, is not to blow my own trumpet but to make a point: don't try to rush things (do a trial assembly, don't just assume the valves won't touch the piston, check it) and don't spoil the ship for a ha'p'orth of tar (don't re-use split pins or tab washer). The rest of this section is going to be a list of things to do and not to do, in no particular order.

I am assuming that you are overhauling the engine at the same time as you are tuning it. So one way of increasing power is to have it rebored to the maximum (usually 0.0060in oversize) which will give you a bit more capacity – as Americans say 'there ain't no substitute for cubic inches'.

Absolute cleanliness is of paramount importance, high pressure air and a lot of cleaning fluid being required as well as clean rags. Lightly oil everything on assembly and clean and prime all oilways.

Don't refit anything that you have any doubts about, it's cheaper in the long run to replace it.

Don't forget to get your connecting rods checked for trueness, bent or twisted rods being one of the most common and biggest power wasters on an engine. If you have any that are distorted they can be straightened but they will probably go back again in time so it's best to replace them.

Even if you can't afford to have the engine balanced (most modern crankshafts are pretty good anyway) you can do the pistons yourself. This won't produce any more power but might make it just a bit smoother and improve the stress life of your engine. Old fashioned kitchen scales are accurate enough for you to get quite close as long as you are careful. Obviously you should only remove metal from unstressed portions of the piston. Purely out of interest, the standard pistons on most engines are the limiting factor on how much power you can safely extract, because of their limited heat dissipation properties and reduced strength at high temperatures.

The crankshaft: not much you can do here except inspect it for cracks and have it reground if necessary. If you are rebuilding an engine that has had a big end go and there is any discolouration on the journal, treat it as scrap if you are going after real performance.

Timing chains or belts are an automatic replacement especially as they form an insignificant part of the cost of the overhaul. Sprockets or gears should be replaced depending on condition at your discretion.

Rockers, pushrods and cam followers must also be judged on condition (cam followers would usually be replaced when fitting a new cam anyway). Likewise the water pump and ancillary drives. However, oil pumps are cheap (relatively) and it's a good insurance to replace that automatically with a new item, preferably an uprated one.

Theoretically, if you can run your engine at a lower temperature it will produce more power (I can hear the howls of protest now, but don't forget I said *theoretically*). Bearing in mind that you will have more heat to dissipate anyway, it's worth looking round your local car breakers for a bigger radiator that will fit your car, and then if possible try and get a thermostat with a lower temperature setting and experiment. Of course, an electric fan is an obvious thing if funds allow.

Whilst on the subject of temperatures, don't forget oil temperature. Some engines even in standard form are marginal in this respect because of the very small amount of oil that is circulating, it doesn't have time even to think about dissipating heat before it's being pumped round again. Unless you are only using your engine for relatively short runs at full power or, if racing, for short events, an oil cooler is a worth while consideration. If that is out of the question then an oil temperature gauge will let you know if things are getting out of hand. I think this is as important as a coolant temperature gauge.

Before you start your engine for the first time, at the very least, with spark plugs removed, pump up oil pressure on the starter. Even better, before you do that, prime the whole engine with a pump type grease gun filled with engine oil through the oil transmitter connection.

Now you have your engine modified, built and running, the next place you should visit (after a short running-in period) is a rolling road. Even experienced mechanics know that it's really the quickest way of setting up a modified engine. The operator can, with your guidance, set the engine up to your requirements. For example it's almost too much to hope that your distributor advance curve will match your engine's requirements under every possible combination of conditions and it's up to you to decide where you want it set for best performance. This even applies to rebuilt distributors: for one to match any engine exactly, it has to be custom built, with the engine on a brake or rolling road, and naturally this tends to be prohibitively expensive for most people.

Engines for competition

If you are building your engine specifically for racing or rallying then all the foregoing instructions apply, but obviously you will not be quite so interested in torque or power at low speed. However, don't forget that an engine which produces power only at mega revs is not necessarily the quickest on the circuit. It's acceleration that wins the races, not top speed, and as acceleration is directly proportional to torque and weight, if the weight stays the same the more usable torque range you have the better your chances are of winning.

Unless you are in a restricted formula you will probably have gone for bigger valves, a racing camshaft, better carburation and be prepared to rebuild your engine more frequently. Also the risk factor will be higher – you will be using a higher rev limit. This means that, apart from the bottom end, which is really beyond this book, a few things change in the head and valve department. Also low speed running is not of great importance.

Firstly a warning: in an attempt to get the maximum flow rate by enlarging the ports it is possible for you to break through into waterways or bolt holes which is, putting it mildly, slightly inconvenient. There is no easy answer to this I'm afraid, because if it happens, the head is basically scrap. Some specialists can repair cylinder heads but because of the very nature of the work it's expensive. It is just feasible on some heads by using various strange and devious devices to measure the wall thickness of the ports. If it's possible on yours and you are worried, then the best advice is to remove only the minimum required even if it means sacrificing some flow (gas can be squeezed through surprisingly tight restrictions if handled properly).

Most of the anti-reversal techniques outlined previously don't interfere with the normal flow; I have mentioned the ones that might and must leave that to your judgment but don't forget about usable revs. On an engine which is to be rebuilt much more often than that of a normal road car, inlet valve guides can with discretion be cut down flush with the port face, also thinner stems can be considered along with even narrower seats if you are using better valves. The exhaust system of a racer, at least if it's an open pipe, should be easier to arrange, allowing you to experiement with different diameters and lengths.

When you are operating at higher gas speeds our beloved 'ratchets' behave in some strange ways. Study **Fig 45 A**, this being a typical inlet manifold to head arrangement. For the moment ignore the changes in pressure and the anti-reversal effect and imagine the gas flowing at fairly high speed. Notice the shape of the streamlines and how at **a** the effective port diameter is slightly smaller than at **b**. The boundary layer at **a** is at lower than mean pressure and possibly turbulent; however, the main flow through the centre is slightly faster than you would expect and if happening at the right time this could be more useful as it keeps the gas speed high.

Now slow the flow down as at **B** and the effect is more pronounced and even better as it can give you more of a usable

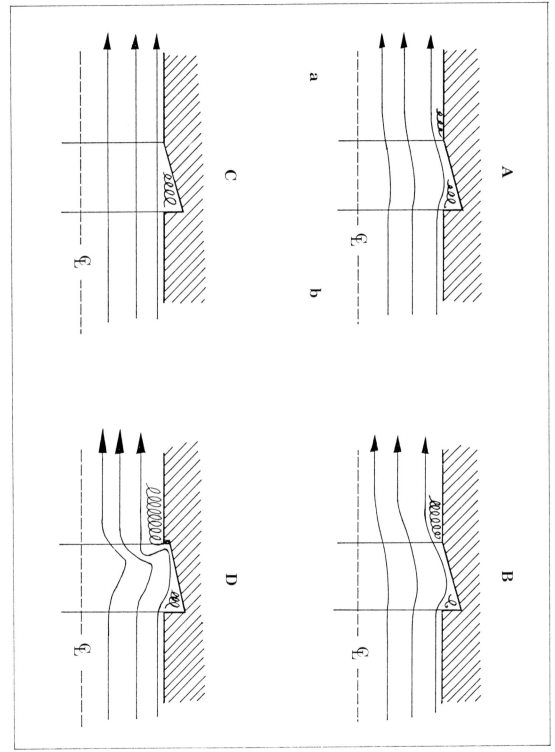

Fig. 45. Effect of anti-reversal 'ratchets' on flow at different gas speeds. The changing shapes of the streamlines indicate how the effective port diameter varies with changes in the behaviour of the boundary layer.

rev range. This of course only really happens when the throttle is wide open, for example when accelerating.

But the really interesting thing happens when we get to **C**: if the gas speed is high enough the boundary layer thins down and a form of shear takes place with the gas flowing straight over the ratchet leaving the pocket relatively stable and therefore not restricting flow.

If you take it one little step further and actually introduce a swirl as in **D** the effect becomes even more pronounced at lower speeds. This can give you a much more tractable engine or allow even more radical cams. It also raises the tantalizing possibility of making use of shock wave effect in the intake system – but that takes us into the realm of advanced aerodynamics and beyond the scope of this book. Besides, I have to keep a few little secrets up my sleeve!

Final diversions

With the possible exception of the anti-reversal systems everything we have considered so far in this book applies just as well if you are fortunate (unfortunate?) enough to have a turbocharger or, better, a supercharger, the only thing that would require different treatment being the compression ratio. Of course you will have to set the cleaner up to blow through the intake, rather than suck, and figure out how to get your probe in the right place, which can be fun. Oh yes, you will also need a pressure gauge as well as a vacuum gauge. Don't forget when using the Plasticine ball method that a restriction will show up as an increase (very slight) in pressure and to measure this you might need to make a longer manometer.

Another thing which your particular engine might have is hydraulic tappets. If you can't get rid of them (some conversion kits are available) then you could have trouble getting accurate actual valve timing figures, the best solution if you have any trouble probably being to get in touch with your camshaft reprofilers and ask for before and after figures.

The almost final point concerns fuel injection. If you have one of the latest all singing and dancing electronic types you shouldn't have any trouble as they will almost all compensate automatically for any improvements you have made. If you have one of the simpler types then you will have little choice but to have it reset when you visit the rolling road, but make sure they really know what they are doing. It's beyond the scope of this book and me to even begin to tell you how to achieve this yourself.

With all this attention focussed on the engine, you could

forget that acceleration, as mentioned earlier, is directly proportional to weight as well as power. If you lose one hundredweight from the car it's nearly equivalent to giving your engine an extra 100cc. But don't lose weight to the detriment of strength or safety.

In conclusion, if there are any blank spots in the book please forgive me. I have tried to explain everything in an understandable way without too much theory. But with one deliberate exception nothing has been intentionally omitted: above all if you test and probe as outlined you will be able to *see* the results even if you don't understand the theory.

Air pollution laws
At the time of writing, checks on the emission of pollutants from the exhausts of individual cars are not yet a legal requirement in the UK. But the situation is more closely controlled in many other countries. By improving the efficiency of an engine, performance tuning may in fact make it cleaner: alternatively it can sometimes have the reverse effect. In carrying out modifications to any car engine, it is important to pay due regard to any emission control regulations which may be in force in your country or state.

ALSO FROM MRP . . .

THEORY AND PRACTICE OF CYLINDER HEAD MODIFICATION. David Vizard. The ideal companion to this book. Intended both as a textbook for the engineering student and as a guide for the practical enthusiast. Imparts much wisdom gathered during the author's many years in the tuning business. Includes actual size drawings of the heads of many popular engines with recommended modifications. 176 pages, 214 x 140mm, approx. 100 illus. Softbound.
0 85113 066 6   £5.95

AUTOMOTIVE GLASSFIBRE. Dennis Foy. A step-by-step handbook for the DIY person who wants to repair, restore, modify or improve the body of a road car, competition car, street machine or special. Covers workshop set-up, tools, materials, techniques, safety and other essentials. 192 pages, 235 x 136mm, 130 illus. Casebound.
0 947981 19 5   £9.95

HANDLING AND ROADHOLDING: CAR SUSPENSION AT WORK. Jeffrey Daniels. Explains clearly and authoritatively the science of chassis performance and the related aspects of car handling, roadholding, ride and response. An important book for all enthusiastic drivers and students of car technology, with many specially executed drawings. 160 pages, 246 x 186mm, approx. 120 illus. Casebound.
0 947981 22 5   £14.95

VOLKSWAGEN PERFORMANCE HANDBOOK. Greg Raven. How to choose, fit, tune and maintain performance equipment for road or track. This is the most thorough book available, covering engine, transmission, suspension and bodywork for all Golf, Rabbit, GTI, Jetta and Scirocco models (1,471cc and larger) from 1974 on. 206 pages, 278 x 215mm, over 400 illus. Softbound.
(Published by Motorbooks International, USA; sole UK distribution by MRP.)
0 87938 268 6   £12.95

RS: THE FASTER FORDS. Jeremy Walton. Acclaimed as the definitive book on the European RS range. Covers all models from Escort RS1600 and Capri RS2600 to the RS200 and the Sierra Cosworth. Skilfully blends production and competition history with quotes from Ford personnel and frank comments from owners. 256 pages, 246 x 186mm, over 250 illus. Casebound.
0 947981 21 7   £14.95

These are just a few examples from the extensive MRP list of tuning and modification books, restoration guides, driving manuals and in-depth model histories, a prime source of interest and information for all motoring enthusiasts. For full details, please write for a free catalogue to:

MOTOR RACING PUBLICATIONS LTD, UNIT 6, THE PILTON ESTATE, 46 PITLAKE, CROYDON, SURREY, CR0 3RY   Telephone 01-681 3363